Microwave Magic
Vegetables

Grolier Limited
TORONTO

Contributors to this series:

Recipes and Technical Assistance:
École de cuisine Bachand-Bissonnette
Cooking consultants:
Denis Bissonette
Michèle Émond
Dietician:
Christiane Barbeau
Photos:
Laramée Morel Communications
Audio-Visuelles
Design:
Claudette Taillefer
Assistants:
Julie Deslauriers
Philippe O'Connor
Joan Pothier
Accessories:
Andrée Cournoyer
Writing:
Communications La Griffe Inc.
Text Consultants:
Cap et bc inc.
Advisors:
Roger Aubin
Joseph R. De Varennes
Gaston Lavoie
Kenneth H. Pearson

Assembly:
Carole Garon
Vital Lapalme
Jean-Pierre Larose
Carl Simmons
Gus Soriano
Marc Vallières
Production Managers:
Gilles Chamberland
Ernest Homewood
Production Assistants:
Martine Gingras
Catherine Gordon
Kathy Kishimoto
Peter Thomlison
Art Director:
Bernard Lamy
Editors:
Laurielle Ilacqua
Susan Marshall
Margaret Oliver
Robin Rivers
Lois Rock
Jocelyn Smyth
Donna Thomson
Dolores Williams
Development:
Le Groupe Polygone Éditeurs Inc.

We wish to thank the following firms, PIER I IMPORTS and LE CACHE POT, for their contribution to the illustration of this set.

The series editors have taken every care to ensure that the information given is accurate. However, no cookbook can guarantee the user successful results. The editors cannot accept any responsibility for the results obtained by following the recipes and recommendations given.

Canadian Cataloguing in Publication Data

Main entry under title:

Vegetables

(Microwave magic ; 13)
Translation of: Les Légumes.
Includes index.
ISBN 0-7172-2434-1

1. Cookery (Vegetables).   2. Microwave cookery.
I. Series: Microwave magic (Toronto, Ont.) ; 13.

TX832.L4313 1988   641.6'5   C88-094212-6

Contents

Note from the Editor.................................. 6

Power Levels.. 7

Garden Fresh Vegetables............................. 8

Buying Vegetables.................................. 10

Seasonal Vegetables................................ 12

Freezing Vegetables................................ 14

Defrosting and Cooking Vegetables.................... 16

Cooking Fresh Vegetables........................... 17

Techniques for Preparing Fresh Vegetables............. 20

Vegetables and the Microwave....................... 26

Recipes... 28

Entertaining....................................... 98

Vegetable Terminology.............................106

Culinary Terms....................................108

Conversion Chart..................................109

Index...110

Microwave Magic is a multi-volume set, with each volume devoted to a particular type of cooking. So, if you are looking for a chicken recipe, you simply go to one of the two volumes that deal with poultry. Each volume has its own index, and the final volume contains a general index to the complete set.

Microwave Magic puts over twelve hundred recipes at your fingertips. You will find it as useful as the microwave oven itself. Enjoy!

Note from the Editor

How to Use this Book
The books in this set have been designed to make your job as easy as possible. As a result, most of the recipes are set out in a standard way.

We suggest that you begin by consulting the information chart for the recipe you have chosen. You will find there all the information you need to decide if you are able to make it: preparation time, cost per serving, level of difficulty, number of calories per serving and other relevant details. Thus, if you have only 30 minutes in which to prepare the evening meal, you will quickly be able to tell which recipe is possible and suits your schedule.

The list of ingredients is always clearly separated from the main text. When space allows, the ingredients are shown together in a photograph so that you can make sure you have them all without rereading the list—

another way of saving your valuable time. In addition, for the more complex recipes we have supplied photographs of the key stages involved either in preparation or serving.

All the dishes in this book have been cooked in a 700 watt microwave oven. If your oven has a different wattage, consult the conversion chart that appears on the following page for cooking times in different types of oven. We would like to emphasize that the cooking times given in the book are a minimum. If a dish does not seem to be cooked enough, you may return it to the oven for a few more minutes. Also, the cooking time can vary according to your ingredients: their water and fat content, thickness, shape and even where they come from. We have therefore left a blank space on each recipe page in which you can note

the cooking time that suits you best. This will enable you to add a personal touch to the recipes that we suggest and to reproduce your best results every time.

Although we have put all the technical information together at the front of this book, we have inserted a number of boxed entries called **MICROTIPS** throughout to explain particular techniques. They are brief and simple, and will help you obtain successful results in your cooking.

With the very first recipe you try, you will discover just how simple microwave cooking can be and how often it depends on techniques you already use for cooking with a conventional oven. If cooking is a pleasure for you, as it is for us, it will be all the more so with a microwave oven. Now let's get on with the food.

The Editor

Key to the Symbols

For ease of reference, the following symbols have been used on the recipe information charts.

The pencil symbol ✏️ is a reminder to write your cooking time in the space provided.

Level of Difficulty

🍴 Easy

🍴🍴 Moderate

🍴🍴🍴 Complex

Cost per Serving

$ Inexpensive

$ $ Moderate

$ $ $ Expensive

Power Levels

All the recipes in this book have been tested in a 700 watt oven. As there are many microwave ovens on the market with different power levels, and as the names of these levels vary from one manufacturer to another, we have decided to give power levels as a percentage. To adapt the power levels given here, consult the chart opposite and the instruction manual for your oven.

Generally speaking, if you have a 500 watt or 600 watt oven you should increase cooking times by about 30% over those given, depending on the actual length of time required. The shorter the original cooking time, the greater the percentage by which it must be lengthened. The 30% figure is only an average. Consult the chart for detailed information on this topic.

Power Levels

HIGH: 100% - 90%	Vegetables (except boiled potatoes and carrots) Soup Sauce Fruits Browning ground beef Browning dish Popcorn
MEDIUM HIGH: 80% - 70%	Rapid defrosting of precooked dishes Muffins Some cakes Hot dogs
MEDIUM: 60% - 50%	Cooking tender meat Cakes Fish Seafood Eggs Reheating Boiled potatoes and carrots
MEDIUM LOW: 40%	Cooking less tender meat Simmering Melting chocolate
DEFROST: 30% **LOW: 30% - 20%**	Defrosting Simmering Cooking less tender meat
WARM: 10%	Keeping food warm Allowing yeast dough to rise

Cooking Time Conversion Chart

700 watts	600 watts*
5 s	11 s
15 s	20 s
30 s	40 s
45 s	1 min
1 min	1 min 20 s
2 min	2 min 40 s
3 min	4 min
4 min	5 min 20 s
5 min	6 min 40 s
6 min	8 min
7 min	9 min 20 s
8 min	10 min 40 s
9 min	12 min
10 min	13 min 30 s
20 min	26 min 40 s
30 min	40 min
40 min	53 min 40 s
50 min	66 min 40 s
1 h	1 h 20 min

* There is very little difference in cooking times between 500 watt ovens and 600 watt ovens.

Garden Fresh Vegetables

For years, the variety of vegetables included regularly in the diets of most North American families was quite limited, with the emphasis mainly on the more common root vegetables such as carrots and potatoes.

Vegetables, however, deserve a more important place. The wide range available to us today, their flavor and nutritional value, and, not least important, their low calorie count are all qualities that should earn them more prominence in the menu planning agenda. They also provide a good source of fiber, which is essential to the digestive system. A healthy, well balanced diet requires vegetables every day.

Now, of course, most vegetables are available throughout the year. And although it was long our custom to overcook them, we have learned to enjoy our vegetables slightly crisp, a quality that maintains both their fresh flavor and their full nutritional value.

The list of different types of vegetables waiting to be sampled is practically endless. Don't stop at lettuce when considering a leafy green vegetable; try spinach, escarole, or chicory. Do yourself a favor and eat artichokes, eggplant, leeks, celeriac, okra and watercress more often. Better yet, if you discover an unknown vegetable at the market bring it home with you—never mind what it looks like. Remember, you are the best judge of what tastes good!

There are also many different families of vegetables. No doubt because they can be kept well past their growing season, root vegetables, or tubers, include some of the most common, such as carrots, beets, turnips, parsnips and potatoes. Another vegetable family frequently found on the table is the cabbage family, which includes green cabbage, cauliflower, broccoli and Brussels sprouts. Then we have the more seasonal vegetables of the grain and pod family, such as corn and beans. Another family is the squash family, which includes zucchini and many types of winter and summer squash. There are a number of varieties in the leafy vegetable family; as well as the different lettuces used in salads, there are spinach, endive and others, which we shall discuss further on. Stem vegetables, such as celery and asparagus; bulb vegetables, such as garlic, onions and leeks; and fruit vegetables, such as tomatoes and peppers, can all be found at the market. Finally, there are mushrooms and artichokes, each forming a separate group.

The next time you go to the green grocer or the supermarket, take a good look at the number of vegetables available. You will find that the choice will amaze you.

Buying Vegetables

Vegetables are very delicate foods. They must be stored carefully so that all their nutritional qualities are preserved. Remember that vegetables lose a great deal of nutritional value if bruised, wilted, or moldy. For example, a wilted leafy vegetable contains practically no Vitamin C. It is therefore important to be very particular when selecting vegetables. These guidelines will help you select those that are the most fresh.

Artichokes: Choose those that are heavy for their size, with firm, stiff, closed leaves. Reject any with opened leaves, a sign that they are overripe. Sometimes the outer leaves of an artichoke that has been exposed to frost may be slightly black; simply remove these leaves.

Asparagus: Look for firm asparagus spears with compact tips. The color may vary from green to white, with tinges of purple.

Beans: Choose medium sized beans that are smooth, crisp and firm.

Beets: Select firm, unblemished beets of uniform size.

Broccoli: Select bunches that are dark green with firm, tender stems and compact heads.

Brussels sprouts: Avoid sprouts with wilted or yellowed leaves, indicating that they are old; choose those with dark green, tight-fitting outer leaves.

Cabbage, green: Choose heads that are heavy for their size, with crisp bright colored leaves, showing no yellow discoloration and no insect blemishes.

Carrots: Choose firm, smooth carrots with no blemishes or green patches. The leaves may be wilted, but make sure that the roots are firm.

Cauliflower: Select creamy white, firm heads, with no blemishes or discoloration, surrounded by crisp leaves which can be used in soups. Do not reject a cauliflower with small leaves sprouting among the flowerets.

Celery: Buy crisp green bunches with straight, unblemished stalks.

Corn: Always make sure that the cobs are cool, even cold, since heat accelerates the transformation of corn sugar into starch. Choose cobs with kernels at the tips and covered with crisp green leaves. The kernels should excrete a white milky juice when pierced.

Endive:	Choose firm, full endives with shiny, unblemished leaves. Store in the dark to prevent them from turning green.
Garlic:	Choose firm garlic buds with dry, white, unblemished skin.
Leeks:	Look for smooth, pale bulbs with crisp tops and relatively long white stalks.
Mushrooms:	Avoid viscous or discolored mushrooms. Select those with short stems, since the cap is the most flavorful part.
Onions:	Select firm onions with dry, brittle skin and no sprouts.
Parsnips:	Buy firm, straight, smooth parsnips with no brown spots.
Peppers:	Select thickly fleshed peppers with firm, smooth skin and no blemishes.
Potatoes:	Choose potatoes with no blemishes or green discoloration, a sign that they contain solanine, a toxic substance. Reject any with sprouts, molds, blemishes, green veins, or too many eyes.
Rutabaga:	Often confused with the turnip, which is smaller and white in color. Look for a firm, heavy rutabaga, with smooth, bright, blemish-free skin.
Spinach:	Choose crisp, clean, dark green colored leaves.
Tomatoes:	Choose firm, thickly fleshed, shiny tomatoes with no wrinkles or cracks. Buy red tomatoes if you wish to eat them immediately.
Vegetable marrow:	Buy pale green vegetable marrow, measuring 10 to 20 cm (4 to 8 in).
Zucchini:	Look for firm zucchini with no signs of blemish or mold.

Seasonal Vegetables

It is always best to eat vegetables when they are fresh and in season. Price is often the best indicator of a vegetable's availability; green peppers are expensive in January and cheaper in August, simply because they are available locally from July to September. However, most of the vegetables described in this book are sold all through the year. Imported vegetables arrive regularly by air and sea, and greenhouses free us from the seasonal constraints that were very limiting not so long ago. It is nonetheless advantageous, both for reasons of freshness and price, to buy vegetables in season. We offer the following guide to help you do so.

Availability of Fresh Vegetables

Vegetable	Season Available
Artichokes	from March to the end of May
Asparagus	from the end of April to the beginning of June
Beans	from July to mid-October
Beets	from July to October
Broccoli	from May to October
Brussels sprouts	from September to the end of November
Cabbage, green	all year, especially in the fall
Carrots	all year
Cauliflower	from August to October
Celery	all year
Corn	from July to mid-September
Endive	from October to May

Availability of Fresh Vegetables

Vegetable	Season Available
Garlic	all year
Leeks	from July to the end of November
Mushrooms	all year
Onions	all year
Parsnips	fall
Peppers	from July to September
Potatoes	all year
Rutabaga	from October to March
Spaghetti squash	summer
Spinach	from June to September
Tomatoes	from May to September
Zucchini	almost all year, especially in the summer

Freezing Vegetables

Good weather brings a profusion of vegetables which, if properly frozen, can be enjoyed all through the winter. Freezing is one of the easiest ways of preserving food, but certain rules do need to be observed. Vegetables should be frozen as quickly as possible after being picked. Always use the freshest and best quality available—while freezing preserves the existing quality of the food it cannot, of course, add quality. First, make sure that the vegetables to be frozen are well cleaned. Most should be blanched. They should then be placed in airtight bags to ensure that they do not dry out by coming into contact with the cold air from the freezer.

Blanching

Blanching is a process that stops the harmful action of the enzymes in vegetables from causing aging and discoloration. Most vegetables require blanching before being frozen.

The traditional method of blanching vegetables is to plunge them into a large pot of boiling water for a few moments and then to transfer them to a tub filled with ice water, so that they cool down and stop cooking immediately.

With a microwave you can shorten the time required to blanch vegetables. Generally, about 450 g (1 lb) of vegetables can be blanched at a time. Fill a dish, equipped with a lid, with between 50 and 75 mL (1/4 to 1/3 cup) of water per 450 g (1 lb) of vegetables. Do not add any salt or seasoning as it may cause dehydration or discoloration. Prepare the vegetables as you normally would for cooking, but cook them for half the normal cooking time (see the table on pages 18 and 19), stirring at least twice during the cooking. The blanched vegetables should have a beautiful, bright color and should still be crisp. Drain them immediately in a colander and then quickly plunge them into ice cold water, until they are completely cool. Drain again and dry the vegetables before wrapping.

Instead of using a dish you may use a freezer bag to cook the vegetables. Prepare the vegetables and place them in the bag with the normal amount of water required for cooking, but again, cook for half the normal time, shaking frequently. Then immerse the bag, up to the top, into ice cold water. While the vegetables are cooling, heat and air will be expelled from the bag, creating a vacuum. When cool, simply seal the bag and freeze.

Wrapping

Before wrapping vegetables for freezing, separate them into portions that are practical for your purposes. Water and odor-proof bags allow for risk-free freezing. Follow the manufacturer's instructions regarding sealing airtight bags. Whenever possible, freeze your vegetables in bags or containers that can be used in the microwave oven. Be sure to label and date the containers clearly. Arrange them side by side in the freezer initially; place one on top of the other only when completely frozen.

Vegetables may be kept for 8 to 12 months in a freezer set at -18°C (0°F) or lower. When you want to use the vegetables, simply cook them as you would any frozen vegetable.

Defrosting and Cooking Frozen Vegetables

Most microwave ovens are equipped with a defrosting feature. In fact, many of the first owners of microwaves used them mainly to speed up the defrosting time of various foods. And indeed, the defrosting process is one more example of how the microwave oven saves you time. Not only does it accelerate the defrosting process, it frequently allows you to skip this stage completely. In many cases, food can be taken directly from the freezer and placed in the microwave oven for cooking.

The table presented on this page gives cooking times for vegetables that you have bought frozen. It will also help you calculate cooking times for vegetables you have frozen yourself, but it is important to realize that the two will not be exactly the same. In both cases, of course, the food has been subjected to very low temperatures in order to preserve it. The food industry, however, uses a very rapid process often referred to as "quick-freezing."

Foods frozen at home will take longer to defrost than quick-frozen foods because the ice crystals formed inside the food during the relatively slower home freezing process are much larger than those formed by quick-freezing. In any case, it is always better to underestimate than to overestimate the time needed to defrost vegetables—better to have to set the defrost feature a second time than to end up with a vegetable that is dehydrated and partially cooked.

Once the vegetable has been defrosted to the point where it can be separated into pieces, cover it with plastic wrap to retain the heat and accelerate the defrosting process. You can also separate the vegetable into pieces and arrange them around other foods you are defrosting.

Cooking Frozen Vegetables

Vegetable	Quantity	Water	Cooking Time at 100% (min)
Asparagus	284 g (10 oz)	—	5 to 6
Beans	284 g (10 oz)	—	4 to 5
Broccoli	284 g (10 oz)	—	5 to 6
Brussels sprouts	284 g (10 oz)	—	5 to 6
Carrots, sliced	284 g (10 oz)	—	5 to 6
Cauliflower, in flowerets	284 g (10 oz)	—	5 to 6
Corn kernels	284 g (10 oz)	—	4 to 5
Spinach	284 g (10 oz)	—	3 to 4
Summer squash, in cubes	284 g (10 oz)	—	5 to 6
Corn on the cob, with leaves	1 each additional cob	— —	3 to 4 1 to 2

Some people prefer to reduce the risk of dehydration by defrosting at 30% power, a slower but safer option. Another solution is simply to watch the vegetables carefully while defrosting and turn them over often. Never allow the vegetables to become completely defrosted as they will dry out and the edges will begin to cook. It is best to remove them from the oven and let the defrosting finish at room temperature.

Whichever way you decide to defrost, be sure to remove the top of the container used to freeze the vegetables. If you have used a plastic bag with a metallic twist-tie, replace the twist-tie with an elastic band, string, or simply close the bag by hand.

To ensure uniform cooking of vegetables being cooked in the bag in which they were frozen, just shake the bag every so often during cooking time.

It is possible to defrost only half a package of frozen vegetables. To do so, simply wrap the unwanted portion of the package in aluminum foil and place the entire package in the oven. Once the unwrapped portion has been defrosted, put the remainder in an airtight container and return to the freezer.

Cooking Fresh Vegetables

In microwave cooking, the food placed around the outer edge of the dish always cooks more quickly than the food at the center. For this reason, any multi-textured vegetable, such as broccoli, should be placed in such a way that the most tender part is at the center of the dish.

Vegetables, even if still slightly firm when pierced with a fork, are properly cooked. Remember that any food continues to cook after it is taken out of the oven. Vegetables should therefore be removed from the oven before they seem completely done and should allowed to stand before being served. Potatoes, for example, require 3 minutes standing time. If you take them out of the oven when they are completely cooked, you will find that they have become dehydrated after the indicated standing time.

For some vegetables, microwave cooking is not necessarily faster than conventional cooking. But it is always best to use a cooking method that preserves the food's nutritional value and, because less water is used in microwave cooking, vegetables are more likely to retain their vitamins. Another advantage to cooking vegetables in the microwave is that the same dish can be used for both cooking and serving—a feature especially appreciated by those whose job it is to wash the dishes!

And, of course, the microwave is definitely the most practical solution when you wish to reheat vegetables quickly.

Cooking Fresh Vegetables

Cooking vegetables in the microwave oven is as simple as it is quick. The following table, containing instructions as to quantity of water needed, cooking times and power levels, shows how to cook some of the most common vegetables. Don't forget to let the vegetables stand once they come out of the oven, allowing the internal heat to be distributed evenly throughout the food.

Vegetable	Quantity	Water	Cooking Time at 100% (min)	Standing Time (min)
Artichokes	6 average	50 mL (1/4 cup) 5 mL (1 teaspoon) lemon juice	10 to 12	3
Asparagus	450 g (1 lb)	50 mL (1/4 cup)	3 to 4-1/2	3
Beans, green	450 g (1 lb)	125 mL (1/2 cup)	9 to 12	3
Beans, lima	450 g (1 lb)	125 mL (1/2 cup)	10 to 13	5
Beets	5 average 450 g (1 lb)	125 mL (1/2 cup)	10 to 12	3
Broccoli, in spears	1 bunch	50 mL (1/4 cup)	4 to 6	3
Brussels sprouts	450 g (1 lb)	30 mL (2 tablespoons)	5 to 6	3
Cabbage, green, in quarters	1 average	50 mL (1/4 cup)	6 to 8	3
Cabbage, green, julienne	500 mL (2 cups)	50 mL (1/4 cup)	4 to 5	3
Carrots, cut in two lengthwise	450 g (1 lb)	125 mL (1/2 cup)	9 to 11	3
Carrots, sliced	450 g (1 lb)	50 mL (1/4 cup)	6 to 8	3
Cauliflower, in flowerets	1 average	50 mL (1/4 cup)	4 to 6	3

Cooking Fresh Vegetables

Vegetable	Quantity	Water	Cooking Time at 100% (min)	Standing Time (min)
Celery, chopped	500 mL (2 cups)	30 mL (2 tablespoons)	3 to 4	3
Corn, on the cob	1	see suggested method*	2 to 4	1
Endive	6	30 mL (2 tablespoons)	4 to 6	3
Leeks	6	50 mL (1/4 cup)	4 to 6	3
Mushrooms	225 g (8 oz)	—	2 to 3	2
Onions, in quarters	4	30 mL (2 tablespoons)	4 to 6	2
Parsnips, in cubes	450 g (1 lb)	50 mL (1/4 cup)	6 to 8	3
Peppers	4	50 mL (1/4 cup)	4 to 6	3
Potatoes, in jackets	2 3 4	— — —	4 to 6 5 to 7 8 to 10	3 3 3
Rutabaga, in cubes	450 g (1 lb)	50 mL (1/4 cup)	7 to 9	3
Spinach	450 g (1 lb)	see suggested method*	3 to 4	2
Summer squash, in cubes	450 g (1 lb)	50 mL (1/4 cup)	4 to 8	3
Tomatoes	1	see suggested method*	2	2
Winter squash, whole	1 average	see suggested method*	8 to 10	3

* See pages 20 to 25 in this volume.

Techniques for Preparing Fresh Vegetables

Equipment
Although the preparation for and microwave cooking of vegetables do not necessarily require any special utensils or dishes, there are some products on the market that may be helpful to you.

For Chopping and Slicing
Many utensils can be used to cut vegetables into slices or cubes rapidly. They replace the kitchen knife but maintain the same level of quality. The vegetable shredder, for example, is equipped with a variety of interchangeable blades and is a very useful kitchen tool.

Another useful tool is the food processor. It is much faster than using a knife, but the vegetables must first be cut by hand to fit into the feeder tube.

For Cooking
Like meat or pasta, vegetables can be served in the same dish that is used to cook them.

Dishes especially designed for cooking vegetables in the microwave oven are available. For example, a 4-litre dish with a double boiler feature is available; the vegetables can be placed so that they do not come into contact with the water during cooking. Other dishes are equipped with special lids that release small amounts of steam during cooking. Such dishes work very well in microwave cooking.

Some containers have hermetic lids and are used to refrigerate cooked vegetables. These lids should not be used for cooking in the microwave oven as they do not allow steam to escape.

Preparation Techniques

Potatoes
Wash and peel the potatoes and cut them into 0.5 cm (1/4 in) cubes. Add water, cover, and cook as directed. Stir once during the cooking time. Let stand for 3 minutes before serving.

Carrots
Wash and trim the carrots. Cut in two lengthwise, or cut across into 0.5 cm (1/4 in) slices. Add water and cover. Cook and let stand for 3 minutes before serving.

Rutabaga
Peel and cut into cubes. Add water and cover. Cook for the time indicated and let stand for 3 minutes before serving.

Beets
If the beets are large, cut them in two to ensure a more rapid and uniform cooking. Wash the beets and trim the ends but do not peel. Add water, cover, and cook. Stir once during the cooking time and let stand for 3 minutes. Drain and then peel them and slice or cut into cubes, as desired.

Brussels Sprouts
Remove any wilted leaves and stems that are too long and wash the sprouts. If necessary, cut the sprouts in two or score the stems by cutting an X into them. Add water and cover. Stir once during the cooking time. Let stand for 3 minutes and drain before serving.

Artichokes
Break off the stem of the artichoke; the stringy part of the base will come away with the stem. Remove the tips of the outside leaves with scissors. The artichokes are cooked when the leaves can be easily detached or when the base can be pierced with a fork. Let stand for 3 minutes before serving.

Broccoli
Wash and separate into individual spears with flowerets. Arrange in a dish with stems pointing outward. Add water, cover and turn the dish halfway through the cooking time. Allow 3 minutes standing time.

Asparagus
Remove the tough ends of the stalks. Wash well. Arrange the asparagus in a dish with the tips toward the center. Cook covered, turning the dish once during the cooking time. Let stand for 3 minutes before serving.

Cauliflower
Wash and trim the cauliflower and separate into flowerets. Add water and cover. Stir once during the cooking time. Let stand for 3 minutes before serving.

Leeks
Remove the fibrous part of the roots and the outside leaves. Cut off the green ends at about 2.5 to 5 cm (1 to 2 in) below the white root ends of the leeks. Cut across into 0.5 cm (1/4 in) slices. Add water, cover, and cook. Stir once during the cooking time. Allow to stand for 3 minutes before serving.

Endive
Use a small knife to make a slit in the root of the endive and remove the bitter center. Detach the leaves and cook covered in water with lemon juice to prevent discoloration. Arrange in a dish with the points toward the center and turn the dish halfway through the cooking time. Let stand for 3 minutes before serving.

Green Beans
Wash and trim the beans. Either cut into 2.5 to 5 cm (1 to 2 in) lengths or leave the beans whole. Add water and cover. Stir once during the cooking time. Let stand covered for 3 minutes before serving. Drain.

Preparation Techniques

Onions
Peel the onions. Add water and cover. Stir once during the cooking time. Let stand covered for 3 minutes before serving. Drain.

Tomatoes
With a paring knife, remove the tough cores of the tomatoes. Pierce the skin before cooking. Let stand for 2 minutes before serving.

Zucchini
Wash the zucchini and cut across 0.5 cm (1/4 in) slices. Add water. Cook covered, and stir once during the cooking time. Drain and let stand for 3 minutes.

Squash
Cut the squash in half or in quarters. Remove the skin and the seeds. Arrange in a baking dish. Add water and cook covered, rearranging the pieces once or twice during the cooking time. Let stand for 3 minutes before serving.

Spinach
Rinse well in a large quantity of cold water and drain. Rinse a second time. Remove the tough stems. Cook the spinach covered, with only the water that is left adhering to the leaves. Stir once during the cooking time. Let stand for 2 minutes before serving.

Peppers
Wash the peppers and cut in half. Remove the seeds and the white membrane and cut into cubes or strips. Add water and cover. Stir once during the cooking time. Let stand for 3 minutes before serving.

Corn on the Cob
If cooking the corn without its leaves, wrap it in waxed paper and twist to close at both ends. If cooking the corn with its leaves, clean it first, remove the silk, and close the leaves. Then pass the cob under running water to add moisture. Cook as directed and let stand for 1 minute before serving.

Mushrooms
Remove the tough ends of the stems. If required, clean the mushrooms before cooking them. Cover and stir once during the cooking time. Let stand for 2 minutes before serving.

Parsnips
Wash and peel the parsnips. Cut lengthwise and then into 1 cm (1/2 in) slices. Add water and cover. Follow the cooking directions and let stand for 3 minutes before serving.

MICROTIPS

For Perfectly Cooked Vegetables
The fresh vegetable cooking guide on pages 18 and 19 shows you how to successfully cook your favorite vegetables in the microwave oven. The first time you cook vegetables in the microwave, however, avoid overcooking. Remember that food can always be cooked longer if necessary but overcooked food cannot be saved. A vegetable that has been exposed to the microwaves for too long will lose moisture and become tough. Follow the instructions given in the cooking guide and carefully observe the standing times, which are a very important part of the cooking cycle.

To accelerate the cooking of such vegetables as potatoes or rutabaga, grate them before putting them into the microwave oven.

Vegetables and the Microwave

Cooking vegetables in the microwave oven offers several advantages over conventional cooking methods. As well as accelerating the cooking time, the microwave oven maintains the nutritional value, the flavor and the color of vegetables.

Microwave cooking requires very little water because the microwaves use the water content in the vegetables to cook them. Additional water is needed only for vegetables that contain very little water, such as carrots, beets and rutabagas. Vegetables containing a great deal of moisture, such as zucchini, mushrooms, spinach and corn on the cob, need no water at all for microwave cooking. The addition of very little water or none at all in vegetable cookery helps preserve the hydrosoluble vitamins (those that dissolve in water). As well, because the microwave oven reduces the cooking time, heat-sensitive vitamins in the

vegetables are also retained. Another advantage in cooking with very little water is that the vegetables retain their crispness and their original flavor. Microwave cooking also ensures that your vegetables will retain their bright colors.

Naturally, the size, temperature and density of the vegetables affect the cooking time; a small potato will cook more rapidly than a large one. Ideally, you should cook vegetables of the same size together. Similarly, cubes, slices or sticks should be as uniform in size as you can make them. Vegetables with more density, such as cauliflower, will take longer to cook than those with less density, such as mushrooms, tomatoes and spinach.

Vegetables, except for potatoes in their jackets, are always cooked in covered containers. In this way, less water is required for cooking and the loss of moisture is reduced.

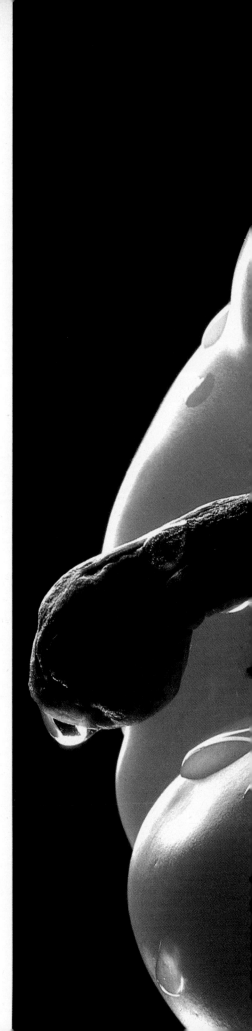

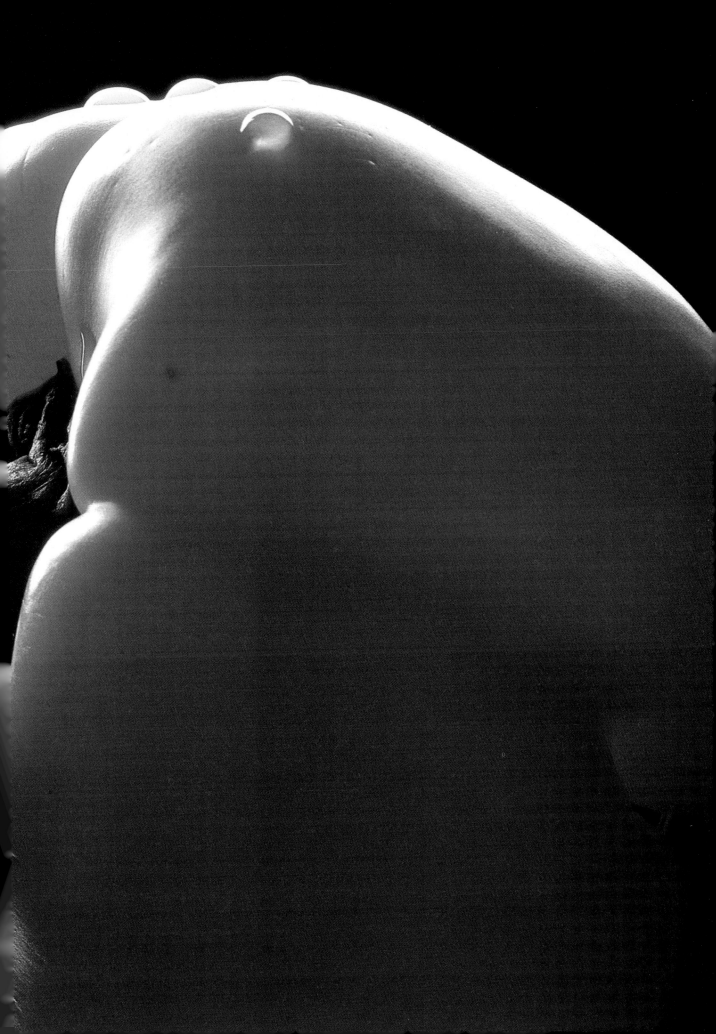

Parsley Potatoes

Level of Difficulty	🍴
Preparation Time	15 min
Cost per Serving	**$**
Number of Servings	10
Nutritional Value	110 calories 1.8 g protein 16.4 g carbohydrate
Food Exchanges	1 bread exchange 1/2 fat exchange
Cooking Time	8 min
Standing Time	None
Power Level	100%
Write Your Cooking Time Here	✏️🍎

Ingredients
900 g (2 lb) small potatoes, whole
50 mL (1/4 cup) water
50 mL (1/4 cup) butter
15 mL (1 tablespoon) parsley, chopped
1 garlic clove, crushed
salt and pepper to taste

Method
— Peel the potatoes.
— Place them in a dish, add the water, cover, and cook at 100% for 4 to 5 minutes.
— Drain the cooking liquid and set the cooked potatoes aside.
— Put the butter, parsley and garlic in another dish and cook at 100% for 1 to 2 minutes.
— Pour this mixture over the potatoes, season with salt and pepper, and heat at 100% for 1 minute.

Serving Suggestions

The delicate flavor of the parsley makes this potato dish an ideal accompaniment for many main courses. The simple ingredients used to prepare it go particularly well with highly seasoned dishes, creating some very interesting taste contrasts.

28

MICROTIPS

Determining Cooking Time for a Mixture of Vegetables

Different vegetables require different cooking times. So what's to be done when cooking a combination of vegetables—for instance, fresh lima beans, potatoes, carrots, and so on? The slowest cooking vegetable determines the cooking time. In this case, the dish should come out of the oven when the lima beans are cooked. If you are not using lima beans, base the cooking time on the length of time needed to cook the potatoes and then the carrots in descending order.

For Best Results

When cooking vegetables in the microwave oven, it is important to ensure that they do not lose moisture during the cooking process. For this reason, peeled or sliced vegetables should be covered. Moreover, vegetables will cook more quickly if covered with a good quality plastic wrap folded back at one corner, or with a lid that releases only a small amount of steam.

Stuffed Potatoes

Level of Difficulty	🍴🍴
Preparation Time	20 min
Cost per Serving	**$**
Number of Servings	6
Nutritional Value	287 calories 20.3 g protein 28.5 g carbohydrate
Food Exchanges	2 oz meat 1-1/2 bread exchanges 1 fat exchange
Cooking Time	17 min
Standing Time	None
Power Level	100%, 70%
Write Your Cooking Time Here	

Ingredients
6 large potatoes, washed but not peeled
175 mL (3/4 cup) milk
50 mL (1/4 cup) green onions, chopped
50 mL (1/4 cup) butter
15 mL (1 tablespoon) parsley, chopped
125 mL (1/2 cup) cheddar cheese, grated
salt and pepper to taste
284 g (10 oz) can of sardines, drained
6 slices of bacon, cooked crisp and crumbled

Method
— Pierce the potatoes with a fork in several places.
— Place them in a dish and cook at 100% for 10 to 12 minutes, giving the dish a half-turn halfway through the cooking time.
— Slice a thin layer of skin off the top of each potato.
— Scoop out the inside of the potato, leaving a 0.5 cm (1/4 in) layer on the inside.
— In a bowl, combine the potato pulp with the milk, green onions, butter, parsley and cheese. Add the seasoning.
— Set 6 sardines aside and crush the others with a fork.
— Add the crushed sardines to the pulp and mix well.
— Stuff each potato with this mixture.
— Sprinkle with the bacon bits and garnish with the whole sardines.
— Arrange the stuffed potatoes on a dish and heat at 70% for 4 to 5 minutes, giving the dish a half-turn midway through the cooking time.

Scoop out the potatoes, leaving a 0.5 cm (1/4 in) layer of pulp on the inside.

Fill the potatoes with the potato pulp mixture and cook as directed in the recipe.

31

Baked Potatoes

Level of Difficulty	🍴🍴
Preparation Time	5 min
Cost per Serving	$
Number of Servings	4
Nutritional Value	93 calories 16 g carbohydrate
Food Exchanges	1 bread exchange 1/2 fat exchange
Cooking Time	8 min
Standing Time	5 min
Power Level	100%
Write Your Cooking Time Here	

Ingredients
4 whole potatoes, washed but not peeled
60 mL (4 tablespoons) sour cream
20 mL (4 teaspoons) chives

Method
— Pierce each potato in several places with a fork.
— Arrange the potatoes in a dish and cook uncovered at 100% for 6 to 8 minutes, giving the dish a half-turn halfway through the cooking time.
— Cover the potatoes with aluminum foil, placing the shiny side against the skin.
— Let stand for 5 minutes.
— Meanwhile, mix the sour cream with the chives.
— Split each potato open with a fork and pour one quarter of the sour cream and chives into the opening.

Potatoes with Veal Stock

Level of Difficulty	🍴
Preparation Time	15 min
Cost per Serving	$
Number of Servings	6
Nutritional Value	160 calories 2.4 g protein 16.1 g carbohydrate
Food Exchanges	1 vegetable exchange 1 bread exchange 1 fat exchange
Cooking Time	6 min
Standing Time	None
Power Level	100%
Write Your Cooking Time Here	

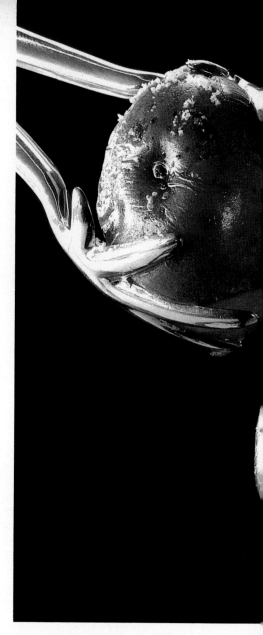

Ingredients
450 g (1 lb) small potatoes, whole
125 mL (1/2 cup) veal stock
1 onion, finely chopped
1 bouquet garni
salt and pepper to taste
50 mL (1/4 cup) oil
15 mL (1 tablespoon) Parmesan cheese, grated

Method
— Wash and partially peel the potatoes.
— Place them in a casserole and add the veal stock. Add the onion and the bouquet garni and season to taste.
— Cook covered at 100% for 4 to 6 minutes, stirring once during the cooking time.
— Remove the potatoes from the casserole and set them aside.
— Preheat a browning dish at 100% for 7 minutes. Pour in the oil and heat at 100% for 30 seconds.
— Sear the potatoes in the oil; sprinkle with the Parmesan cheese before serving.

Serving Suggestions
These potatoes, cooked in veal stock, are a delicious accompaniment to most meat dishes. Your guests will especially enjoy them with a roast or with a succulent steak.

Assemble the ingredients required for this dish, in which the flavor of the veal stock is delicately blended with that of the potatoes.

Partially peel the potatoes before cooking.

Sear the potatoes in oil in the preheated browning dish and sprinkle with Parmesan cheese.

Scalloped Potatoes

Level of Difficulty	
Preparation Time	20 min
Cost per Serving	$
Number of Servings	8
Nutritional Value	159 calories 59 g protein 13 g carbohydrate
Food Exchanges	1/2 oz meat 1 bread exchange 1/4 milk exchange 1/2 fat exchange
Cooking Time	18 min
Standing Time	10 min
Power Level	100%
Write Your Cooking Time Here	

Ingredients

1 L (4 cups) whole potatoes, washed and peeled
45 mL (3 tablespoons) flour
5 mL (1 teaspoon) salt
250 mL (1 cup) cheddar cheese, grated
0.5 mL (1/8 teaspoon) celery seed
175 mL (3/4 cup) milk
50 mL (1/4 cup) 18% cream
30 mL (2 tablespoons) butter
2 mL (1/2 teaspoon) paprika

Method

— Cut the potatoes into thin slices.
— In a bowl, combine the flour, salt, grated cheddar cheese and celery seed; set aside.
— Pour the milk and cream into a measuring cup, heat at 100% for 2 to 3 minutes, and set aside.
— Place half the sliced potatoes in a baking dish and sprinkle with half of the flour and cheese mixture.
— Add the remaining potato slices and sprinkle with the rest of the flour and cheese.
— Pour the milk and cream over the potatoes, dot with bits of the butter, and sprinkle with the paprika.
— Cook uncovered at 100% for 13 to 15 minutes, or until the potatoes are tender, giving the dish a half-turn halfway through the cooking time.
— Let stand for 10 minutes before serving.

Serving Suggestions
Prepared in this way, scalloped potatoes make a fairly substantial dish. They can accompany many meat dishes, but it is best to serve them with relatively light ones.

Place half the potatoes in a casserole and sprinkle them with half of the flour and cheese mixture.

Add the remaining potatoes, top with more flour and cheese, and pour the heated mixture of milk and cream over the potatoes. Cook as directed.

"Two-Step" Potatoes

Level of Difficulty	🍴🍴
Preparation Time	20 min
Cost per Serving	$
Number of Servings	8
Nutritional Value	194 calories 6.2 g protein 19 g carbohydrate
Food Exchanges	1 oz meat 1 bread exchange 1 fat exchange
Cooking Time	19 min
Standing Time	2 x 3 min
Power Level	100%
Write Your Cooking Time Here	

MICROTIPS

For Perfectly Cooked Potatoes

Potatoes may not feel tender after the suggested cooking time. They are nonetheless ready to remove from the oven. The internal heat will be uniformly distributed and the cooking cycle completed during the standing time. At the end of this standing period, the potatoes will be completely cooked and tender.

Ingredients
4 large potatoes, washed but not peeled
125 mL (1/2 cup) plain yoghurt
50 mL (1/4 cup) green onions, chopped
125 mL (1/2 cup) orange cheddar cheese, grated
125 mL (1/2 cup) Gruyère cheese, grated
50 mL (1/4 cup) butter
salt and pepper to taste

Method
— Pierce the potatoes in several places with a fork.
— Place them in a dish and cook at 100% for 9 to 11 minutes.
— Let stand for 3 minutes.
— Cut each potato, lengthwise, in half.
— Scoop out the potato pulp, leaving a 0.5 cm (1/4 in) layer on the inside to keep the shell stiff.
— In a bowl combine the scooped out pulp, the yoghurt, green onions, half the cheddar cheese, the Gruyère cheese and the butter; season to taste.
— Stuff each potato half with the mixture and cook at 100% for 4 to 6 minutes.
— Give the dish a half-turn and top with the remaining cheddar cheese.
— Continue to cook at 100% for 1 to 2 minutes.
— Let stand for 3 minutes before serving.

Potatoes with Onions

Level of Difficulty	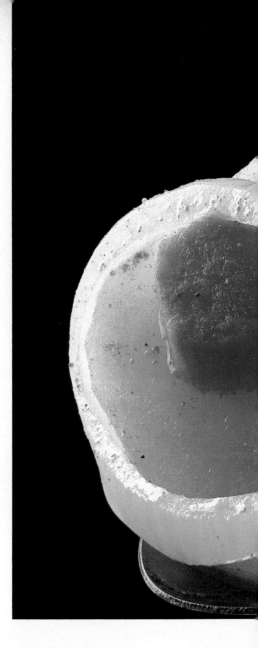 (utensils icon)
Preparation Time	20 min
Cost per Serving	$
Number of Servings	4
Nutritional Value	116 calories 2.8 g protein 20.8 g carbohydrate
Food Exchanges	1 vegetable exchange 1 bread exchange 1/2 fat exchange
Cooking Time	11 min
Standing Time	5 min
Power Level	100%
Write Your Cooking Time Here	

Ingredients
4 medium potatoes
2 carrots
1 onion
45 mL (3 tablespoons) butter
salt and pepper to taste
celery salt and paprika to
taste

Method
— Wash and peel the
  vegetables and cut into
  slices.
— Melt the butter at 100%
  for 1 minute.
— Arrange the sliced
  vegetables in a dish, pour
  in the melted butter,
  cover, and cook at 100%
  for 8 to 10 minutes,
  stirring halfway through
  the cooking time.
— Add the seasoning to
  taste.
— Let stand for 5 minutes
  before seving.

Serving Suggestions
Potatoes with onions may be
served with most beef, veal
and lamb dishes. They may
also be served with any
highly flavored meat dish.

Assemble the ingredients needed to prepare this tasty and original combination of vegetables.

Slice the vegetables after washing and peeling them.

Pour the melted butter into the dish over the vegetables before cooking them.

41

Three-Vegetable Garnish

Level of Difficulty	
Preparation Time	20 min
Cost per Serving	$
Number of Servings	12
Nutritional Value	97 calories
Food Exchanges	3 vegetable exchanges 1/2 fat exchange
Cooking Time	8 min
Standing Time	3 min
Power Level	100%
Write Your Cooking Time Here	

Ingredients
675 g (1-1/2 lb) zucchini, thinly sliced
675 g (1-1/2 lb) carrots, grated
675 g (1-1/2 lb) rutabaga, grated
75 mL (1/3 cup) butter
125 mL (1/2 cup) water
15 mL (1 tablespoon) sugar

Method
— In a large casserole, melt the butter at 100% for 1 minute.
— Add the water and sugar and cook at 100% for 2 minutes.
— Add the vegetables and mix well.
— Cover the casserole and cook at 100% for 4 to 5 minutes, stirring once halfway through the cooking time.
— Let stand for 3 minutes before serving.

⇒

Three-Vegetable Garnish

Zucchini, carrots and rutabaga are the star ingredients of this delicious vegetable garnish.

Add the vegetables to the water, sugar and melted butter and mix well.

Cover the casserole and cook at 100% for 4 to 5 minutes, stirring once halfway through the cooking time to ensure uniform cooking.

MICROTIPS
Making Smaller Quantities

To prepare half the amount of a recipe, the amount of each ingredient should obviously be reduced by one half. Similarly, to convert a 4-serving recipe into a single serving, divide the quantity of ingredients by 4. Be sure to use a proportionately smaller cooking dish.

For a recipe cut in half, reduce the original cooking time by approximately a third. To prepare one-quarter of a recipe, cook for one-third of the suggested time. Check the degree of doneness periodically.

Follow the instructions for preparation and handle the ingredients as indicated in the original recipe.

Pay special attention to such details as the initial temperature of the ingredients, which affect the cooking process. Foods with a high fat or sugar content tend to cook quickly. The standing time may be reduced slightly or, in most cases, left as in the original recipe.

Glazed Carrots

Ingredients

450 g (1 lb) carrots, cut into sticks
50 mL (1/4 cup) water

30 mL (2 tablespoons) butter
30 mL (2 tablespoons) brown sugar, packed
15 mL (1 tablespoon) honey

1 mL (1/4 teaspoon) ground ginger
salt and pepper to taste

Level of Difficulty	🍴
Preparation Time	20 min
Cost per Serving	$
Number of Servings	8
Nutritional Value	68 calories
Food Exchanges	2 vegetable exchanges 1/2 fat exchange
Cooking Time	10 min
Standing Time	3 min
Power Level	100%
Write Your Cooking Time Here	

Method

— Place the carrots in a dish, add the water, cover, and cook at 100% for 6 to 8 minutes, stirring once after 4 minutes.
— Let stand for 3 minutes, drain, and set aside.
— Combine all the other ingredients in a bowl and heat at 100% for 1 to 2 minutes, stirring once halfway through the cooking time.
— Pour the glaze over the carrots before serving.

Carrots with Cream

Level of Difficulty	
Preparation Time	10 min
Cost per Serving	$
Number of Servings	8
Nutritional Value	101 calories
Food Exchanges	2 vegetable exchanges 1 fat exchange
Cooking Time	11 min
Standing Time	None
Power Level	100%
Write Your Cooking Time Here	

Ingredients
450 g (1 lb) small carrots, whole
15 mL (1 tablespoon) butter
50 mL (1/4 cup) water
15 mL (1 tablespoon) dried herbs (parsley or a mixture of parsley, chervil, tarragon and chives)
salt and pepper to taste
125 mL (1/2 cup) 35% cream
3 egg yolks

Method
— Combine the carrots, butter, water and the seasoning in a dish.
— Cover and cook at 100% for 5 minutes.
— Add the cream, stir and continue to cook for 5 to 6 minutes longer; set aside.
— In a bowl, beat the egg yolks while adding a small quantity of the cream sauce in which the carrots were cooked.
— Pour the beaten egg mixture over the carrots and blend into the sauce.
— Mix well until the sauce is smooth and serve immediately.

Serving Suggestions
This classic carrot dish is certain to be a success. It may be served with all your favorite meat dishes, but it is particularly well suited to poultry.

These are the ingredients you will need to prepare this recipe.

Add the cream between the two stages of cooking.

Beat the egg yolks, incorporating some of the cream sauce from the carrots. Pour the egg mixture over the carrots and blend into the cream sauce.

Beets with Vinegar

Level of Difficulty	🍴
Preparation Time	20 min
Cost per Serving	$
Number of Servings	10
Nutritional Value	51 calories
Food Exchanges	2 vegetable exchanges
Cooking Time	14 min
Standing Time	5 min
Power Level	100%
Write Your Cooking Time Here	

Ingredients
675 g (1-1/2 lb) beets, peeled and sliced
15 mL (1 tablespoon) cornstarch
75 mL (1/3 cup) cold water
15 mL (1 tablespoon) butter, melted
75 mL (1/3 cup) vinegar
50 mL (1/4 cup) sugar

Method
— Dissolve the cornstarch in the cold water and set aside.
— Combine the melted butter, vinegar, sugar and the dissolved cornstarch in a dish and mix well.
— Cook at 100% for 2 minutes to thicken the sauce, stirring once during the cooking time.
— Add the beets to the sauce, cover, and cook at 100% for 12 minutes, stirring twice during the cooking time.
— Let stand for 5 minutes before serving.

Serving Suggestions
Beets with vinegar are always appreciated. Their tartness goes particularly well with braised dishes and stews as well as with roast pork.

Beet Ketchup

Ingredients
675 g (1-1/2 lb) beets, peeled and grated
15 mL (1 tablespoon) butter
250 mL (1 cup) vinegar
250 mL (1 cup) sugar
15 mL (1 tablespoon) pickling spice
30 mL (2 tablespoons) cornstarch
50 mL (1/4 cup) cold water

Method
— Combine the beets, butter, vinegar, sugar and pickling spice in a dish and mix well.
— Cover and cook at 100% for 8 to 10 minutes, stirring twice during the cooking time.
— Dissolve the cornstarch in the cold water and add it to the beet mixture.
— Continue to cook at 100% for 4 to 6 minutes, stirring twice during the cooking time.
— Let stand for 15 minutes and transfer the beet ketchup to jars.

Mixed Vegetables

Level of Difficulty	🍴
Preparation Time	20 min
Cost per Serving	**$**
Number of Servings	16
Nutritional Value	60 calories
Food Exchanges	2 vegetable exchanges
Cooking Time	22 min
Standing Time	3 min
Power Level	100%
Write Your Cooking Time Here	

Ingredients
250 mL (1 cup) carrots, thinly sliced across
500 mL (2 cups) broccoli flowerets
500 mL (2 cups) cauliflower flowerets
50 mL (1/4 cup) water
50 mL (1/4 cup) butter
2 mL (1/2 teaspoon) rosemary
15 mL (1 tablespoon) red pepper, roasted and chopped
50 mL (1/4 cup) Parmesan cheese, grated

Method
— Place the carrots in a dish, add the water, cover, and cook at 100% for 7 minutes, stirring after 4 minutes.
— Add the broccoli and the cauliflower, cover, and cook at 100% for 10 to 12 minutes, stirring once during the cooking time.
— Allow to stand, covered, for 3 minutes. Drain.
— Melt the butter at 100% for 1 minute and add the rosemary and the chopped red pepper.
— Pour the butter mixture over the vegetables and sprinkle with the Parmesan cheese.
— Heat at 100% for 2 minutes and serve.

$\Rightarrow$

Mixed Vegetables

This delicious mixture of vegetables may be served with most main courses. Here are the ingredients needed to prepare the recipe.

Pour the water over the carrots. Cover and cook at 100% for 7 minutes, stirring after 4 minutes.

Add the broccoli and the cauliflower. Cover and continue to cook as directed in the recipe.

At the end of the standing time, use a colander to drain the vegetables.

Add the rosemary and red pepper to the melted butter and pour over the vegetables.

Sprinkle with the Parmesan cheese and heat at 100% for 2 minutes.

MICROTIPS

For a Quick Meal

Whether you buy packaged TV dinners at the supermarket or keep your own prepared meals in the freezer, the microwave oven enables you to produce meals in a hurry.

If the meal has been frozen in its package (usually a disposable aluminum foil tray), place it on a microwave-safe serving plate and heat as directed. Your meal will be ready in an instant.

If you prefer your own recipes, simply prepare them as usual, divide them into three or four portions, and freeze them in freezer-to-oven dishes. When you are caught short of time, simply take the dish from the freezer and pop it into the microwave oven. You will have a nourishing meal in minutes!

Rutabaga and Green Pepper with Cheese

Ingredients
1 rutabaga, diced
75 mL (1/3 cup) water

50 mL (1/4 cup) butter
250 mL (1 cup) green pepper, chopped

50 mL (1/4 cup) onion, chopped
30 mL (2 tablespoons) flour
125 mL (1/2 cup) chili sauce
salt and pepper to taste
50 mL (1/4 cup) cheddar cheese, grated
paprika to garnish

Level of Difficulty	🍴
Preparation Time	20 min
Cost per Serving	**$**
Number of Servings	6
Nutritional Value	137 calories
Food Exchanges	2 vegetable exchanges 2 fat exchanges
Cooking Time	15 min
Standing Time	None
Power Level	100%
Write Your Cooking Time Here	

Method
— Place the diced rutabaga in a dish, add the water, cover and cook at 100% for 6 to 7 minutes, stirring once; set aside.
— Heat the butter at 100% for 1 minute, add the green pepper and onion, and cook at 100% for 1 minute.
— Sprinkle with the flour, add the chili sauce, salt and pepper and cook at 100% for 3 to 4 minutes, stirring halfway through the cooking time.
— Add the rutabaga and the cheddar cheese to the dish, mix, and sprinkle with paprika.
— Heat at 100% for 2 minutes before serving.

Cabbage Quiche

Level of Difficulty	
Preparation Time	20 min
Cost per Serving	**$**
Number of Servings	6
Nutritional Value	336 calories 8.5 g protein 13.3 g carbohydrate
Food Exchanges	1 oz meat 2 vegetable exchanges 1 bread exchange 3 fat exchanges
Cooking Time	22 min
Standing Time	4 min
Power Level	70%, 100%
Write Your Cooking Time Here	

Ingredients
1 quiche crust
500 mL (2 cups) green cabbage, grated
75 mL (1/3 cup) butter
250 mL (1 cup) 10% cream
3 eggs
salt and pepper to taste
50 mL (1/4 cup) Parmesan cheese, grated
50 mL (1/4 cup) Gruyère cheese, grated
paprika to garnish

Method
— Place the quiche crust in a pie plate and cook on a rack at 70% for 5 to 6 minutes, giving the plate a half-turn halfway through the cooking time. Set aside.
— Put the grated cabbage in a dish, cover and cook at 100% for 3 to 4 minutes; drain carefully and set aside.
— Melt the butter at 100% for 1 minute and add the cream and the eggs.
— Beat with a whisk, season to taste and set aside.
— Fill the quiche crust with the cooked cabbage, cover with the egg and cream mixture, and sprinkle with the grated cheeses and the paprika.
— Put the pie plate on a rack in the microwave oven and cook at 70% for 9 to 11 minutes, giving the dish a half-turn halfway through the cooking time.
— Let stand for 4 minutes before serving.

Assemble the ingredients needed for this savory, easy-to-prepare recipe.

Bake the quiche crust on a raised rack at 70% for 5 to 6 minutes, giving the dish a half-turn halfway through the cooking time.

Broccoli and Ham Casserole

Level of Difficulty	🍴
Preparation Time	20 min
Cost per Serving	$
Number of Servings	4
Nutritional Value	397 calories 21.2 g protein 21.4 g carbohydrate
Food Exchanges	2 oz meat 2 vegetable exchanges 1 bread exchange 1/2 milk exchange
Cooking Time	32 min
Standing Time	None
Power Level	100%, 70%
Write Your Cooking Time Here	

Ingredients
500 mL (2 cups) broccoli flowerets
250 mL (1 cup) ham, cut in cubes
1.55 L (6-1/4 cups) water
250 mL (1 cup) macaroni, uncooked
75 mL (5 tablespoons) butter
45 mL (3 tablespoons) flour
500 mL (2 cups) milk
salt and pepper to taste
5 mL (1 teaspoon) prepared mustard
125 mL (1/2 cup) cheddar cheese, grated

Method
— To cook the macaroni, bring 1.5 L (6 cups) of water to the boil by heating at 100% for 6 to 8 minutes; add 30 mL (2 tablespoons) of the butter and the macaroni; cook at 100% for 5 to 7 minutes, stirring once halfway through the cooking time.
— Pour the cooked macaroni into a colander, drain and rinse with cold water; put the macaroni into a baking dish and set aside.
— Put the broccoli flowerets into a dish and add the remaining 50 mL (1/4 cup) water; cook at 100% for 4 to 5 minutes, stirring once during the cooking time; drain well and set aside.
— Prepare a béchamel sauce by first melting the remaining 45 mL (3 tablespoons) of butter at 100% for 30 to 40 seconds; add the flour and mix well; stir in the milk and cook at 100% for 6 to 8 minutes, stirring every 2 minutes.
— Season the béchamel sauce to taste, add the mustard and mix well.

— Combine the cubed ham and the cooked broccoli with the sauce and pour over the macaroni.
— Sprinkle with the cheddar cheese, reduce the power to 70%, and cook for 2 to 4 minutes, giving the dish a half-turn halfway through the cooking time.

Assemble the ingredients needed to prepare this tasty dish.

MICROTIPS

For Uniform Cooking

For evenly cooked vegetables be sure to place the thicker parts of the vegetable toward the outside of the dish. If several different types of vegetables are being cooked together, put the faster cooking vegetables in the center of the dish.

Broccoli with Almonds

Ingredients

450 g (1 lb) fresh broccoli,
cut into spears
50 mL (1/4 cup) water

1 mL (1/4 teaspoon) sugar
30 mL (2 tablespoons) butter
30 mL (2 tablespoons)
blanched almonds, sliced

10 mL (2 teaspoons) lemon
juice
salt and pepper to taste

Level of Difficulty	🍴🍷
Preparation Time	10 min
Cost per Serving	$
Number of Servings	4
Nutritional Value	106 calories
Food Exchanges	2 vegetable exchanges 1 fat exchange
Cooking Time	10 min
Standing Time	3 min
Power Level	100%
Write Your Cooking Time Here	🍎✏️

Method

— Put the broccoli in a dish,
add the water and sugar,
and cook covered at 100%
for 4 to 6 minutes, stirring
halfway through the
cooking time.
— Let stand for 3 minutes,
drain and set aside.
— To prepare the almond
garnish, first melt the
butter at 100% for 1
minute; add the almonds,
stir well and brown at
100% for 2 to 3 minutes,
stirring halfway through
the cooking time. If the
almonds are not
sufficiently browned, cook
for 1 minute longer.
— Add the lemon juice, salt
and pepper and pour over
the cooked broccoli.

Brussels Sprouts with Mushrooms

Ingredients
20 to 24 Brussels sprouts
1 onion, finely chopped
50 mL (1/4 cup) water

225 g (8 oz) mushrooms, cut in half
45 mL (3 tablespoons) butter

15 mL (1 tablespoon) lemon juice
salt and pepper to taste

Method
— Put the Brussels sprouts and the onion in a dish and add the water; cover and cook at 100% for 6 to 8 minutes; drain and let stand for 3 minutes.
— In another dish cook the mushrooms in the butter at 100% for 1 to 2 minutes; add the lemon juice and season.
— Pour the mushrooms over the Brussels sprouts and serve immediately.

Level of Difficulty	🍴
Preparation Time	10 min
Cost per Serving	$
Number of Servings	8
Nutritional Value	57 calories
Food Exchanges	1 vegetable exchange 1/2 fat exchange
Cooking Time	10 min
Standing Time	3 min
Power Level	100%
Write Your Cooking Time Here	

Cauliflower à la Polonaise

Ingredients
1 head cauliflower, separated into flowerets
45 mL (3 tablespoons) water
salt and pepper to taste
50 mL (1/4 cup) breadcrumbs
2 hard-boiled eggs, chopped

Method
— Put the cauliflower flowerets in a dish, add the water, cover and cook at 100% for 4 to 6 minutes; drain and let stand for 3 minutes.

— Add salt and pepper to taste and sprinkle the breadcrumbs and the chopped egg over the cauliflower before serving.

Brussels Sprouts with Sour Cream

Ingredients
1 L (4 cups) Brussels sprouts
50 mL (1/4 cup) water
250 mL (1 cup) sour cream
30 mL (2 tablespoons) onion, finely chopped
30 mL (2 tablespoons) roasted red pepper, chopped
salt and pepper to taste

Method
— Put the Brussels sprouts in a dish, add the water, cover and cook at 100% for 6 to 8 minutes, stirring once during the cooking time.
— Let stand for 3 minutes.
— In the meantime, prepare the sauce by combining all the other ingredients and heat at 50% for 1 minute.
— Drain the Brussels sprouts and coat with the sauce before serving.

Yellow Beans Creole Style

Ingredients
675 g (1-1/2 lb) yellow beans
75 mL (1/3 cup) water
30 mL (2 tablespoons) butter
50 mL (1/4 cup) onion,
chopped
50 mL (1/4 cup) celery,
chopped
75 mL (1/3 cup) chili sauce

Method
— Put the beans in a dish
and add the water; cover
and cook at 100% for 10
to 12 minutes, stirring
halfway through the
cooking time; set aside.
— In another dish, heat the
butter at 100% for 2 to 3
minutes, stirring once
during the cooking time.
— Pour the sauce over the
beans, mix well, and heat
at 100% for 2 minutes.

Level of Difficulty	🍴
Preparation Time	15 min
Cost per Serving	$
Number of Servings	10
Nutritional Value	56 calories
Food Exchanges	2 vegetable exchanges
Cooking Time	17 min
Standing Time	None
Power Level	100%
Write Your Cooking Time Here	

Green Beans with Tomato Sauce

Level of Difficulty	
Preparation Time	20 min
Cost per Serving	$
Number of Servings	12
Nutritional Value	87 calories
Food Exchanges	1 vegetable exchange 1-1/2 fat exchanges
Cooking Time	14 min
Standing Time	4 min
Power Level	100%
Write Your Cooking Time Here	

Ingredients
450 g (1 lb) green beans
75 mL (1/3 cup) water
50 mL (1/4 cup) butter
2 onions, chopped
125 mL (1/2 cup) green pepper, finely chopped
3 tomatoes, peeled and chopped
5 mL (1 teaspoon) basil
1 egg
250 mL (1 cup) sour cream
salt and pepper to taste

Method
— Place the green beans in a dish and add the water; cover and cook at 100% for 9 to 10 minutes, stirring halfway through the cooking time.
— Let stand for 4 minutes.
— In the meantime, heat the butter in another dish at 100% for 1 minute and add the onions, green pepper, tomatoes, and basil. Cook at 100% for 2 to 3 minutes, stirring once during the cooking time.
— Beat the egg, stirring in the sour cream, and add to the onion, green pepper, and tomato mixture. Season with salt and pepper.
— Drain the beans and coat with the sauce before serving.

Serving Suggestions
The delicate flavor of the beans, enhanced by the sharpness of the tomatoes, accompanies roast pork and most chicken dishes very well.

Assemble these ingredients to prepare this interesting recipe for green beans.

To make the sauce, add the onions, green pepper, tomatoes and basil to the melted butter. Cook as directed and then add the egg and sour cream.

MICROTIPS

About Salt

We do not recommend that salt be added to vegetables before cooking them in the microwave oven. Salt hastens the dehydration process and should not be added to the vegetables directly. If you must add salt, add it to the water in which the vegetables are to be cooked.

Corn with Chili Sauce

Level of Difficulty	🍴
Preparation Time	5 min
Cost per Serving	$
Number of Servings	6
Nutritional Value	98 calories 16 g carbohydrate
Food Exchanges	2 vegetable exchanges 1 fat exchange
Cooking Time	10 min
Standing Time	None
Power Level	100%
Write Your Cooking Time Here	🍎✏️

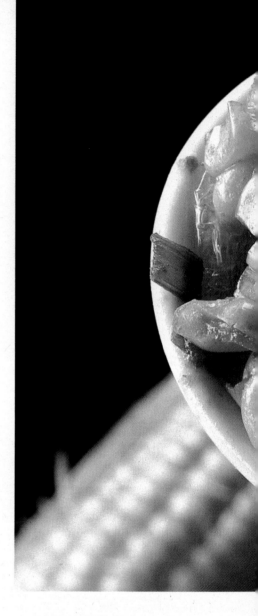

Ingredients
375 mL (1-1/2 cups) corn, in kernels
150 mL (2/3 cup) chili sauce
50 mL (1/4 cup) green onions, chopped
30 mL (2 tablespoons) butter

Method
— Combine all the ingredients in a dish and mix well.
— Cover and cook at 100% for 5 minutes, until the mixture reaches the boiling point, and stir.
— Continue to cook at 100% for 4 to 5 minutes, stirring once during the cooking time.

Serving Suggestions

This dish is ideal as part of a quick meal because it can be prepared in a jiffy. Why not serve it with a ground beef casserole or with an omelette?

MICROTIPS

Preparing Frozen Foods Quickly

You can save time by cooking frozen vegetables in their original packaging —providing, of course, that the package is microwave safe.

Frozen Vegetables in a Box:

Remove the vegetables from the carton or the aluminum tray and cook them in a polyethylene bag.

Frozen Vegetables in a Bag:

Cut a hole in the center of the bag and cook the vegetables according to the manufacturer's directions. When cooking is completed, slit the bag open from the hole.

Ratatouille

Level of Difficulty	🍴
Preparation Time	20 min
Cost per Serving	$
Number of Servings	8
Nutritional Value	67 calories
Food Exchanges	2 vegetable exchanges
Cooking Time	15 min
Standing Time	5 min
Power Level	100%
Write Your Cooking Time Here	

Ingredients
1 medium eggplant, sliced
2 medium zucchini, sliced
1 green pepper, cut into large dice
4 fresh tomatoes, cut into quarters
2 onions, cut into large dice
2 cloves garlic, chopped
2 mL (1/2 teaspoon) basil
pinch savory
salt and pepper to taste
50 mL (1/4 cup) Parmesan cheese, grated
45 mL (3 tablespoons) oil
parsley, chopped, to garnish

Method
— Combine all the ingredients, except the Parmesan cheese and parsley, in a 2 L (8 cup) microwave-safe casserole.
— Mix well, cover and cook at 100% for 12 to 15 minutes, stirring halfway through the cooking time.
— Sprinkle with the Parmesan cheese and parsley.
— Let stand for 5 minutes before serving.

Stuffed Zucchini

Level of Difficulty	
Preparation Time	20 min
Cost per Serving	$
Number of Servings	3
Nutritional Value	266 calories 10.7 g protein
Food Exchanges	1 oz meat 2 vegetable exchanges 3 fat exchanges
Cooking Time	10 min
Standing Time	None
Power Level	100%
Write Your Cooking Time Here	

Ingredients
3 medium zucchini
30 mL (2 tablespoons) butter
30 mL (2 tablespoons) fresh parsley, chopped
15 mL (1 tablespoon) olive oil
15 mL (1 tablespoon) onion, finely chopped
1 clove garlic, thinly sliced
1 medium tomato, chopped
125 mL (1/2 cup) fine breadcrumbs
30 mL (2 tablespoons) Parmesan cheese, grated
salt and pepper to taste
pinch cayenne pepper
125 mL (1/2 cup) mozzarella cheese, grated
paprika to garnish

Method
— Cut each zucchini in half, lengthwise.
— Remove the pulp, leaving a 0.5 cm (1/4 in) layer on the inside of the shell.
— Place the zucchini shells in a rectangular dish and set aside.
— In a bowl, combine the butter, parsley, oil, onion and garlic and mix well.
— Heat at 100% for 1 1/2 to 2 minutes, until the butter is melted. Add the zucchini pulp, tomato, breadcrumbs, Parmesan cheese, salt, pepper and cayenne and stir until evenly mixed.

— Fill the zucchini shells with the stuffing, cover the dish, and cook at 100% for 4 to 6 minutes, giving the dish a half-turn halfway through the cooking time.
— Remove the cover, sprinkle the zucchini with the mozzarella cheese and paprika and continue to cook at 100% for 1 to 2 minutes.

To save time when preparing this recipe, first assemble all the required ingredients.

Fill the zucchini shells with the prepared stuffing and cook as directed in the recipe.

Zucchini Italian Style

Level of Difficulty	🍴
Preparation Time	15 min
Cost per Serving	**$**
Number of Servings	6
Nutritional Value	107 calories
Food Exchanges	2 vegetable exchanges 1 fat exchange
Cooking Time	12 min
Standing Time	5 min
Power Level	100%
Write Your Cooking Time Here	

Ingredients
5 to 6 zucchini
30 mL (2 tablespoons) oil
4 to 5 stalks celery, diced
125 mL (1/2 cup) Italian-style tomato sauce
5 mL (1 teaspoon) sugar
1 mL (1/4 teaspoon) garlic salt
2 mL (1/2 teaspoon) salt
1 mL (1/4 teaspoon) oregano
30 mL (2 tablespoons) Parmesan cheese, grated
30 mL (2 tablespoons) Italian breadcrumbs

Method
— Cut the zucchini across into 0.5 cm (1/4 in) slices.
— Combine the sliced zucchini, oil, celery, tomato sauce and the seasoning in a dish and mix well.
— Sprinkle with the Parmesan cheese and breadcrumbs, cover, and cook at 100% for 10 to 12 minutes, giving the dish a half-turn halfway through the cooking time.
— Let stand for 5 minutes before serving.

Serving Suggestions

Lovers of Italian food will enjoy serving this flavorful dish with veal scallopini.

Zucchini prepared in this way also go well with fillets of fish and with most omelettes.

70

Assemble these ingredients to prepare this delicious zucchini recipe.

Cut the zucchini across into 0.5 cm (1/4 in) slices.

Sprinkle the combined ingredients with Parmesan cheese and breadcrumbs before cooking.

71

Spinach Purée

Level of Difficulty	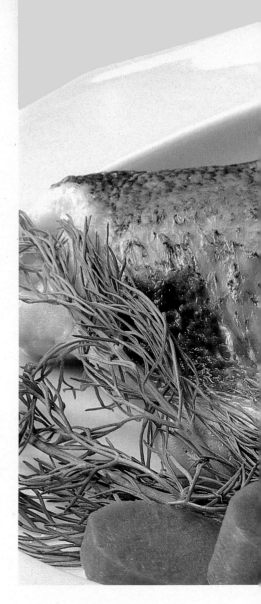
Preparation Time	10 min
Cost per Serving	$
Quantity	375 mL (1 1/2 cups), or approximately 8 servings
Nutritional Value	44 calories
Food Exchanges	1 vegetable exchange 1/2 fat exchange
Cooking Time	4 min
Standing Time	None
Power Level	100%
Write Your Cooking Time Here	

Ingredients
450 g (1 lb) fresh spinach
125 mL (1/2 cup) milk
45 mL (3 tablespoons) 18%
cream
125 mL (1/2 cup) chicken
broth
10 mL (2 teaspoons) melted
butter
pinch nutmeg
salt and pepper to taste

Method
— Clean the spinach, put
  into a dish, cover, and
  cook at 100% for 3 to 4
  minutes.
— Drain carefully in a
  colander.
— Put the spinach into a
  blender or food processor
  and add the milk, cream
  and chicken broth.
— Blend at high speed, add
  the melted butter, and
  season to taste.
— Blend to obtain an even
  consistency.

Serving Suggestions

Not everyone is fond of the
strong flavor of spinach.
However, many people will
be agreeably surprised by the
flavor of this spinach purée,
softened by the addition of
the other ingredients. It goes
well with poached fish,
seafood or poultry dishes.

Assemble the few ingredients needed for this spinach purée.

Cook the spinach in a covered dish to retain the moisture released during cooking.

Drain the spinach in a colander before combining it with the other ingredients.

Tomato Ketchup

Level of Difficulty	🍴
Preparation Time	45 min
Cost per Serving	**$**
Quantity	2.5 L (10 cups)
Nutritional Value	25 calories per 15 mL (1 tablespoon)
Food Exchanges	1 vegetable exchange per 15 mL (1 tablespoon)
Cooking Time	1 h 30 min
Standing Time	None
Power Level	100%
Write Your Cooking Time Here	✏️

Ingredients
10 red tomatoes
10 green tomatoes
6 red onions
750 mL (3 cups) vinegar
1 L (4 cups) sugar
60 mL (4 tablespoons) pickling spice

Method
— Peel all the tomatoes, cut into quarters, drain, and place in a 4 L (16 cup) microwave-safe casserole.
— Slice the onions and add them to the tomatoes.
— Wrap the pickling spice in cheesecloth and place it in the casserole with all the other ingredients.
— Cook uncovered at 100% for 1 to 1-1/2 hours, stirring every 15 minutes.
— Remove the pickling spice and store the ketchup in small containers.

Tomatoes Provençale

Level of Difficulty	🍴
Preparation Time	5 min
Cost per Serving	$
Number of Servings	4
Nutritional Value	139 calories
Food Exchanges	1 vegetable exchange 1/4 bread exchange 2 fat exchanges
Cooking Time	4 min
Standing Time	None
Power Level	100%
Write Your Cooking Time Here	

Ingredients
4 fresh tomatoes
salt and pepper to taste
45 mL (3 tablespoons) butter
1 clove garlic, chopped
75 mL (1/3 cup) Italian breadcrumbs

Method
— Cut the tomatoes in half horizontally and place in a dish; add salt and pepper and set aside.
— In a small bowl combine the butter, garlic and breadcrumbs and heat at 100% for 1 minute, until the butter is melted.
— Top the tomatoes with the mixture and cook uncovered at 100% for 2 to 3 minutes, giving the dish a half-turn halfway through the cooking time.

Serving Suggestions

Served with veal, seafood or roast beef, these tomatoes are sure to earn you many compliments.

Served as an appetizer or as part of the main course, tomatoes provençale are always appreciated. Only a few ingredients are needed to prepare them.

Use a sharp knife to cut the tomatoes in half horizontally.

Arrange the tomatoes in a dish and top with the mixture of butter, garlic and breadcrumbs before cooking.

Onion and Tomato Casserole

Level of Difficulty	🍴
Preparation Time	20 min
Cost per Serving	$
Number of Servings	8
Nutritional Value	181 calories 10.7 g protein 14.7 g carbohydrate
Food Exchanges	1 oz meat 2 vegetable exchanges 1/4 bread exchange 1 fat exchange
Cooking Time	17 min
Standing Time	None
Power Level	100%
Write Your Cooking Time Here	

Ingredients
450 g (1 lb) onions, sliced
4 large tomatoes, sliced
45 mL (3 tablespoons) butter
125 mL (1/2 cup) Italian breadcrumbs
1 mL (1/4 teaspoon) paprika
1 mL (1/4 teaspoon) parsley, chopped
salt and pepper to taste
5 mL (1 teaspoon) basil
6 to 8 slices of cheese, as desired

Method
— Put the onions in a dish, cover and cook at 100% for 4 minutes, stirring once during the cooking time; set aside.
— In a bowl combine the butter, breadcrumbs, paprika and parsley; heat at 100% for 1 minute and set aside.
— In a casserole arrange one layer of cooked onions, cover with a layer of tomatoes, and season with salt, pepper and basil. Spread half the cheese slices on top.
— Continue with another layer of onions, a layer of tomatoes and a layer of cheese.
— Spread the top with the breadcrumb mixture and cook uncovered at 100% for 10 to 12 minutes.

Assemble all the ingredients needed for this savory, easy-to-prepare recipe.

MICROTIPS

Combine the butter, breadcrumbs, paprika and parsley and heat at 100% for 1 minute. Top the casserole, once assembled, with this mixture.

To Defrost Small Servings of Vegetables

It is possible to defrost only half a package of frozen vegetables. Simply wrap the unwanted portion of the package in aluminum foil and place the package in the microwave oven. Heat at 30%. When the unwrapped portion is defrosted, put the remaining vegetables in an airtight container and return to the freezer.

Stuffed Pepper Canapés

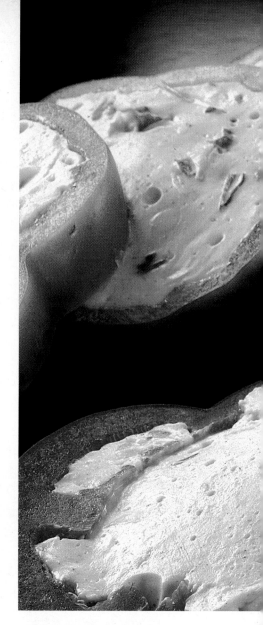

Level of Difficulty	🍴
Preparation Time	15 min*
Cost per Serving	$
Number of Servings	8
Nutritional Value	91 calories
Food Exchanges	1 vegetable exchange 1 1/2 fat exchanges
Cooking Time	3 min
Standing Time	None
Power Level	100%
Write Your Cooking Time Here	

* The stuffed peppers should be refrigerated for 24 hours before serving.

Ingredients
1 green pepper
1 red pepper
175 g (6 oz) cream cheese
2 green onions, thinly sliced
30 mL (2 tablespoons) 18%
cream
salt and pepper to taste
paprika to taste

Method
— Wash the peppers, remove the stem and core with a sharp knife; scoop out the seeds and white membrane.
— Put the peppers in a dish, cover and heat at 100% for 2 to 3 minutes.
— Drain the peppers and let cool.
— Meanwhile, combine the cream cheese, green onions, cream and seasoning in a bowl and blend well until the mixture is creamy.
— Stuff the peppers with the mixture and chill for 24 hours in the refrigerator.
— Cut each pepper, across into 8 slices. Serve on toast as an hors d'oeuvre.

These stuffed peppers make a delicious hors d'oeuvre. First assemble all the ingredients required.

Remove the stem of the pepper with a sharp knife and scoop out the inside.

Stuff the peppers with the cream cheese mixture and refrigerate for 24 hours before serving.

Tomato Mousse

Ingredients
900 g (2 lb) tomatoes, peeled and chopped
2 green onions, thinly sliced
75 mL (1/3 cup) white wine
150 mL (2/3 cup) chicken broth

salt and pepper to taste
1 package unflavored gelatin
5 mL (1 teaspoon) lemon juice
125 mL (1/2 cup) 35% cream

Method
— Cook the green onions at 100% for 2 minutes.
— Add the white wine, chicken broth, tomatoes, salt and pepper; cook uncovered at 100% for 15 to 20 minutes, breaking up the tomatoes after 10 minutes.
— Dissolve the gelatin in water and add to the tomato mixture.
— Pour the mixture into a blender or food processor and purée.
— Strain through a sieve and add the lemon juice.
— Refrigerate until the mixture begins to set.
— Whip the cream and fold it into the partially set tomato mixture.
— Pour the mousse into a greased mold and refrigerate for several hours before serving.

Level of Difficulty	🍴🍴
Preparation Time	20 min*
Cost per Serving	**$**
Number of Servings	10
Nutritional Value	68 calories
Food Exchanges	2 vegetable exchanges 1/2 fat exchange
Cooking Time	22 min
Standing Time	None
Power Level	100%
Write Your Cooking Time Here	

* The mousse should be refrigerated for several hours before serving.

Casserole of Artichokes and Peas

Ingredients
1 398 mL (14 oz) can of
artichoke hearts, drained
500 mL (2 cups) frozen peas
1 onion, chopped

30 mL (2 tablespoons) butter
1 red pepper, cut into strips
salt and pepper to taste
15 mL (1 tablespoon) parsley,
chopped

Method
— Put the onion and butter
in a dish and cook at
100% for 2 minutes.
— Add the artichoke hearts,
peas, and red pepper
strips. Season with salt
and pepper, cover and
cook at 100% for 4 to 5
minutes, stirring gently
halfway through the
cooking time.
— Garnish with the chopped
parsley before serving.

Level of Difficulty	🍴
Preparation Time	10 min
Cost per Serving	$
Number of Servings	8
Nutritional Value	87 calories 13 g carbohydrate
Food Exchanges	2 vegetable exchanges 1/2 fat exchange
Cooking Time	7 min
Standing Time	None
Power Level	100%
Write Your Cooking Time Here	

Stuffed Artichokes

Level of Difficulty	🍴🍴
Preparation Time	25 min
Cost per Serving	$
Number of Servings	6
Nutritional Value	157 calories
Food Exchanges	1 oz meat 1 vegetable exchange 1 fat exchange
Cooking Time	8 min
Standing Time	3 min
Power Level	100%
Write Your Cooking Time Here	

Ingredients
6 artichokes
50 mL (1/4 cup) bread, crumbled
125 mL (1/2 cup) Parmesan cheese, grated
1 medium onion, chopped
2 cloves garlic, crushed
30 mL (2 tablespoons) parsley, chopped
90 mL (6 tablespoons) oil
50 mL (1/4 cup) water

Method
— Combine the bread, Parmesan cheese, onion, garlic and parsley. Mix well and set aside.
— Remove the stems of the artichokes and trim the tip of each leaf.
— Spread the leaves at the top of each artichoke and fill with the bread stuffing.
— Sprinkle each artichoke with 15 mL (1 tablespoon) of oil.
— Place the artichokes in a dish with the water, cover and cook at 100% for 7 to 8 minutes, giving the dish a half-turn halfway through the cooking time.
— Check that the artichokes are properly cooked by pricking with a fork; if the fork slides in easily cooking is completed; if not, continue to cook for another minute.
— Let stand for 3 minutes before serving.

Artichoke and Mushroom Salad

Level of Difficulty	
Preparation Time	10 min*
Cost per Serving	$
Number of Servings	8
Nutritional Value	170 calories
Food Exchanges	2 vegetable exchanges 2-1/2 fat exchanges
Cooking Time	None
Standing Time	None
Power Level	None
Write Your Cooking Time Here	

* The salad should be refrigerated for 3 to 4 hours before serving.

Ingredients
450 g (1 lb) artichoke hearts
450 g (1 lb) mushrooms, sliced
125 mL (1/2 cup) oil
75 mL (1/3 cup) lemon juice
15 mL (1 tablespoon) sugar
10 mL (2 teaspoons) salt
5 mL (1 teaspoon) Dijon mustard
1 clove garlic, crushed
30 mL (2 tablespoons) red pepper, chopped

Method
— Drain the artichoke hearts and set aside.
— Combine the oil, lemon juice, sugar, salt, mustard and garlic and mix well.
— Add the artichoke hearts, mushrooms and red pepper to the dressing, cover and refrigerate for 3 to 4 hours, stirring occasionally.

Serving Suggestions

Serve this salad in the summer as a main course or as a side dish for a special dinner. All your guests will congratulate you.

This salad is easy to make and can be prepared quickly. First, assemble the required ingredients.

Combine all the ingredients needed to prepare the vinaigrette dressing.

Add the artichoke hearts, mushrooms and red pepper to the dressing and refrigerate.

Fried Vegetables Chinese Style

Level of Difficulty	🍴
Preparation Time	20 min
Cost per Serving	$
Number of Servings	4
Nutritional Value	135 calories
Food Exchanges	3 vegetable exchanges 1-1/2 fat exchanges
Cooking Time	3 min
Standing Time	5 min
Power Level	100%
Write Your Cooking Time Here	

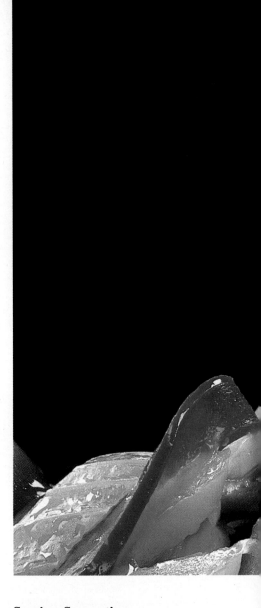

Ingredients
45 mL (3 tablespoons) oil
250 mL (1 cup) celery, sliced on the bias
1 onion, cut into large dice
250 mL (1 cup) green pepper, cut into strips
125 mL (1/2 cup) red pepper, cut into strips
250 mL (1 cup) mushrooms, sliced
1 package of chow mein sauce mix

Method
— Preheat a browning dish at 100% for 7 minutes, add the oil, and heat at 100% for 30 seconds.
— Put all the vegetables into the dish, cover and cook at 100% for 2 to 3 minutes.
— Let stand for 5 minutes and then stir in the chow mein sauce, heated, before serving.

Serving Suggestions

Serve these vegetables with Chinese-style beef or chicken dishes for a delicious mixture of flavors that you will want to create again and again.

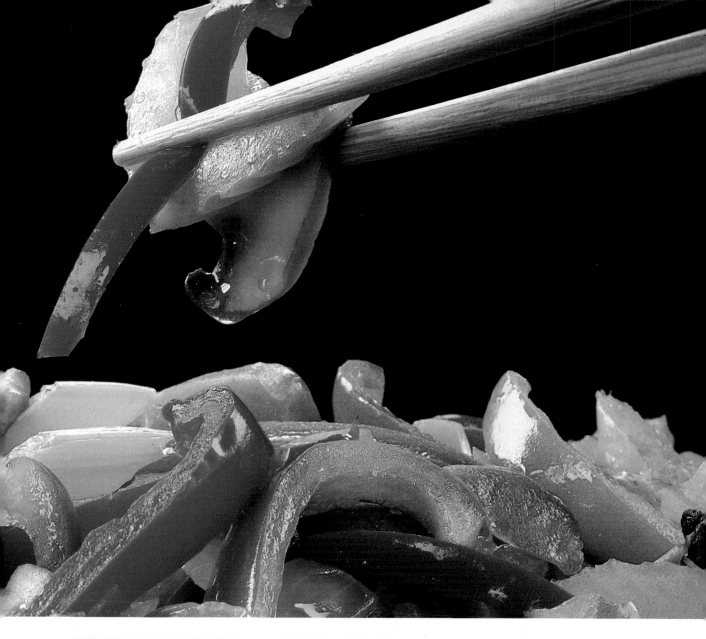

This quick and easy dish is an original way to prepare vegetables. These are the ingredients you will need.

Add all the vegetables to the hot oil and cook covered at 100% for 2 to 3 minutes.

MICROTIPS

To Clarify Butter

Put 50 mL (1/4 cup) of butter in a glass microwave-safe dish and heat at 100% for 1 to 1-1/2 minutes. Remove the clear fat from the surface and discard the milky liquid at the bottom.

89

Asparagus with Almonds

Level of Difficulty	🍴🔪
Preparation Time	10 min
Cost per Serving	$ $
Number of Servings	4
Nutritional Value	100 calories
Food Exchanges	1 vegetable exchange 1-1/2 fat exchanges
Cooking Time	7 min
Standing Time	3 min
Power Level	100%
Write Your Cooking Time Here	🍎✏️

Ingredients
225 g (8 oz) asparagus
30 mL (2 tablespoons) water
45 mL (3 tablespoons) butter
slivered almonds, to taste
22 mL (1-1/2 tablespoons) lemon juice
fresh parsley, chopped

Method
— Place the asparagus in a dish with the water and cook, covered, at 100% for 3 to 4 minutes.
— Let stand covered for 2 to 3 minutes.
— In a bowl, melt the butter at 100% for 40 seconds; add the almonds and cook at 100% for 3 minutes until golden, stirring once during the cooking time.
— Add the lemon juice and mix well.
— Pour the butter, almonds and lemon juice over the asparagus and garnish with parsley before serving.

Serving Suggestions

Asparagus with almonds is a delicately flavored dish, which may be served with beef, veal, lamb, pork or chicken.

Try it also with poached fillets of fish for a very subtle taste combination.

MICROTIPS

To Keep Endive from Discoloring During Cooking

Endive will turn brown if cooked in water alone and will appear much less appetizing, although the flavor is not affected. To avoid this unattractive result, we advise that you soak the endive leaves in cold water mixed with lemon juice before cooking.

If you don't have time to soak the leaves, you can obtain satisfactory results by adding some lemon juice to the cooking water. Be sure to first detach the leaves or cut the endive in half.

Stuffed Onions

Level of Difficulty	
Preparation Time	30 min
Cost per Serving	$
Number of Servings	4
Nutritional Value	221 calories 17.3 g protein 14.2 g carbohydrate
Food Exchanges	1.5 oz meat 3 vegetable exchanges 1 fat exchange
Cooking Time	39 min
Standing Time	5 min
Power Level	100%
Write Your Cooking Time Here	

Ingredients
4 large onions, peeled
50 mL (1/4 cup) water
4 slices of bacon
225 g (8 oz) veal, minced
50 mL (1/4 cup) mushrooms, sliced
15 mL (1 tablespoon) breadcrumbs
2 tomatoes, peeled, chopped and drained
salt and pepper to taste

Method
— To blanch the onions, place them in a dish with the water, cover, and cook at 100% for 5 to 6 minutes, giving the dish a half-turn halfway through the cooking time.
— Cool the onions by rinsing them under cold water.
— Remove the central core of each onion; chop the cores finely and set aside.
— Place the bacon slices on a rack and cook at 100% for 3 to 4 minutes.
— Crumble the cooked bacon slices and set aside.
— Cook the minced veal in the bacon fat at 100% for 3 to 4 minutes, breaking up the meat with a fork twice during the cooking time.
— Add the mushrooms, breadcrumbs, tomatoes, bacon and chopped onion to the veal and season to taste.
— Fill the onions with this stuffing and arrange them in a dish.
— Cover and cook at 100% for 20 to 25 minutes, giving the dish a half-turn halfway through the cooking time.
— Let stand for 5 minutes before serving.

After blanching the onions, remove the central cores and set the shells aside.

Chop the onion cores finely and add to the mushroom, breadcrumb, tomato, bacon and veal stuffing.

Fill the onions with the stuffing, place them in a dish, cover, and cook as directed in the recipe.

93

Leek Flan

Level of Difficulty	
Preparation Time	15 min
Cost per Serving	**$**
Number of Servings	6
Nutritional Value	278 calories 14 g protein
Food Exchanges	2 oz meat 1 vegetable exchange 1-1/2 fat exchanges 1/4 milk exchange
Cooking Time	21 min
Standing Time	3 min
Power Level	100%, 70%
Write Your Cooking Time Here	

Ingredients
8 leeks
50 mL (1/4 cup) water
6 eggs
175 mL (3/4 cup) milk
250 mL (1 cup) 35% cream
175 mL (3/4 cup) breadcrumbs
salt and pepper to taste
150 mL (2/3 cup) cheddar cheese, grated

Method
— Cut the leeks into 5 cm (2 in) slices across, put the slices into a dish and add the water.
— Cover and cook at 100% for 4 to 5 minutes; drain and set aside.
— Beat the eggs in a bowl and add the milk, cream, breadcrumbs and seasoning.
— Add the beaten egg mixture to the leek slices.
— Place the dish on a rack in the microwave oven and cook at 70% for 11 to 13 minutes, stirring after 4 minutes and giving the dish a half-turn after 6 minutes.
— Add the cheddar cheese; increase the power to 100% and continue to cook, uncovered, for 2 to 3 minutes, giving the dish a half-turn halfway through the cooking time.
— Let stand for 3 minutes before serving.

Cut the leeks into 5 cm (2 in) slices before cooking them in a little water.

Beat the eggs and add the milk, cream and breadcrumbs before pouring over the leek slices.

MICROTIPS

To Defrost Bread

Simply place the bread, with its packaging open, in the microwave oven and heat at 20% for 1 to 1-1/2 minutes, until the ice crystals are no longer visible. Let stand for 5 minutes and then remove the bread from its packaging. Cut the bread or separate the slices and let stand for 5 to 10 minutes at room temperature.

Summer Vegetable Combination

Level of Difficulty	
Preparation Time	20 min
Cost per Serving	$
Number of Servings	10
Nutritional Value	87 calories
Food Exchanges	2 vegetable exchanges 1/2 fat exchange
Cooking Time	20 min
Standing Time	5 min
Power Level	100%
Write Your Cooking Time Here	

Ingredients
4 bacon slices
12 pearl onions
1 green pepper, cut into large dice
75 mL (1/3 cup) water
15 mL (1 tablespoon) sugar
450 g (1 lb) green beans, cut in two
6 zucchini, sliced
2 celery stalks, chopped
1 large tomato, cut into thick slices

Method
— Arrange the bacon slices on a rack and cook at 100% for 3 to 4 minutes; crumble and set aside.
— Cook the onions and the green pepper in the bacon fat at 100% for 3 to 4 minutes.
— Add the water, sugar, green beans, zucchini and celery; cover and continue to cook at 100% for 10 to 12 minutes, stirring halfway through the cooking time.
— Add the tomato slices and let stand for 5 minutes.
— Arrange the cooked vegetables on a platter and garnish with the bacon bits before serving.

Cook the onions and the green pepper in the bacon fat.

Add the water, sugar and remaining vegetables and stir halfway through the cooking time to ensure even cooking.

MICROTIPS

To Reheat Foods That Cannot Be Stirred

Certain types of foods cannot be stirred during cooking or reheating. To ensure that they are heated uniformly, pivot the dish a few times while reheating.

Entertaining

Menu:
Lentil Soup
Green Salad
Tofu Quiche
Fruit and Pecan Tart

Fruit and vegetables are part of Mother Nature's bounty. Season after season, year after year, we enjoy the abundance of her products, which provide us with the nutritional elements we need for healthy, well balanced diets.

If the friends and family who share your table are not already confirmed vegetable lovers, they surely will be after you introduce them to the delights of a meal based entirely on vegetables and cooked in the microwave oven. The menu we suggest for entertaining is certain to satisfy the most demanding of palates.

With lentil soup as the first course you will discover, if you don't already know, all the qualities of this very nutritious vegetable, one with exceptional energy-giving value. A green salad follows—easy to prepare and always enjoyed, it adds an indispensable refreshing touch to the meal. Some of your guests may want to eat the salad on its own and others may prefer to have it with the main course.

The tofu quiche we offer as the main course is based on an ingredient that is widely used in oriental cooking and that is becoming increasingly popular in North America. This quiche recipe also includes broccoli and cheddar cheese. Finally, a fruit and pecan tart completes this sumptuous dinner.

From the Recipe to Your Table

Unfortunately, there is no such thing as an instant feast. Preparing a meal for a special occasion when many guests are invited requires a certain amount of thought and organization. Cooking a complete meal in the microwave oven must be planned ahead in the same way as a meal cooked in a conventional oven. Only the cooking and reheating times vary.

8 hours before the meal:
—Prepare the fruit and pecan tart.
3 hours before the meal:
—Prepare the vinaigrette.
2 hours before the meal:
—Prepare the lentil soup.
45 minutes before the meal:
—Prepare the green salad.
30 minutes before the meal:
—Prepare the tofu quiche.

Lentil Soup

Ingredients
300 mL (1 1/4 cups) red lentils
1.25 L (5 cups) hot water
2 potatoes, cubed
1 onion, chopped
1 carrot, thinly sliced
2 cloves garlic, crushed
30 mL (2 tablespoons) parsley, chopped
5 mL (1 teaspoon) salt
5 mL (1 teaspoon) cumin

Method
— Rinse the lentils well, until the water runs perfectly clear.
— Combine all the ingredients in a large casserole and mix well.
— Cover and cook at 100% for 20 to 30 minutes, stirring once during the cooking time.

Information about Lentils
Long disdained and considered peasant fare, lentils have not enjoyed many "highs" historically. Their qualities, however, are currently being examined more carefully in dietary terms. Lentils, in fact, are quite rich in a number of energy-giving minerals and vitamins, such as potassium (388 mg per 250 mL or 1 cup), phosphorus, iron and the B vitamins. For this reason, we have learned to use them in purées, salads and, above all, in soups. We are sure that all your guests will enjoy this recipe.

Tofu Quiche

Ingredients
450 g (1 lb) plain tofu
50 mL (1/4 cup) oil
2 mL (1/2 teaspoon) turmeric
pinch sea salt
pinch thyme
15 mL (1 tablespoon) lemon
juice
375 mL (1 1/2 cups) broccoli
flowerets
1 onion, finely chopped
250 mL (1 cup) old cheddar
cheese, grated
paprika to garnish

Method
— Combine the tofu, oil,
  turmeric, salt, thyme and
  lemon juice in a blender
  and blend at high speed
  until creamy.
— Put the broccoli and
  chopped onion in a dish
  with a little water, cover
  and cook at 100% for 3 to
  4 minutes.
— Combine the cooked
  vegetables with the tofu
  mixture and pour into a
  quiche mold.
— Top with grated cheddar
  cheese and sprinkle with
  paprika.
— Cook the quiche on a rack
  at 70% for 10 to 12
  minutes, giving the dish a
  half-turn halfway through
  the cooking time.
— Let stand for 3 minutes
  before serving.

Green Salad

Ingredients

Salad:
Boston lettuce
romaine lettuce
green onions, as desired
radishes, as desired
sunflower seeds, as desired

Vinaigrette:
75 mL (1/3 cup) lemon juice
150 mL (2/3 cup) oil
2 mL (1/2 teaspoon) sugar
2 mL (1/2 teaspoon) dry mustard
1 egg yolk
1 clove garlic, cut in two
30 mL (2 tablespoons) 18% cream
salt and pepper to taste

Method

— First prepare the vinaigrette by combining all the ingredients except the oil in a bowl and whisk well. Incorporate the oil slowly, whisking until creamy.
— Refrigerate for 3 hours.
— To prepare the salad, detach the lettuce leaves, rince under cold water, dry carefully, and tear into pieces.
— Slice the green onions and the radishes and toss well with the lettuce leaves.
— Pour the vinaigrette over the salad 5 minutes before serving.
— Sprinkle with sunflower seeds just before serving.

About Lettuce

There are four major varieties of lettuce: iceberg, Boston, romaine and leaf. Although iceberg lettuce is the most popular of the four, probably because of its crispness, the other varieties are more nutritious.

Lettuce is mainly eaten raw, in different kinds of salads. It may, however, be cooked lightly, as is the case in some classic French dishes.

The table below, drawn from data provided by Health and Welfare Canada *(Nutrient Value of Some Common Foods),* shows the large amount of water content found in lettuce as well as its high mineral count.

Lettuce	Unit of Measurement	Weight g	Water %	Energy calories	Calcium mg	Potassium mg
leaves	2 large	50	94	10	34	132
cut into pieces	250 mL (1 cup)	78	96	10	16	137

Fruit and Pecan Tart

Ingredients
250 mL (1 cup) pecans, finely chopped
30 mL (2 tablespoons) maple syrup
60 mL (4 tablespoons) whole wheat flour
50 mL (1/4 cup) grated coconut
15 mL (1 tablespoon) sesame butter (Tahini)
a variety of fresh fruit, as desired
15 mL (1 tablespoon) sugar
30 mL (2 tablespoons) cornstarch
125 mL (1/2 cup) apple juice

Method
— In a bowl combine the pecans, maple syrup, flour, coconut and sesame butter; mix well, until smooth.
— Coat a tart mold with an anti-stick agent.
— Pour the mixture into the mold and spread evenly.
— Cook on a rack at 70% for 2 to 3 minutes, giving the dish a half-turn halfway through the cooking time. Allow to cool.
— Fill the mold with a variety of fresh fruit and sprinkle with sugar.
— Dissolve the cornstarch in the apple juice and heat at 100% for 2 minutes, stirring once during the cooking time.
— Pour the glaze over the tart.

Let Your Imagination Be Your Guide

There is nothing nicer than presenting your guests with a fresh fruit tart, using a variety of ripe, seasonal fruits. Any combination of fruit is allowed—let your imagination inspire you! The recipe above does not specify any particular fruit to be used in the dish; so feel free to use whatever you like and create tarts from very traditional to the most innovative.

Try replacing apples with a less traditional choice: pears, for example, or quince, for a truly original variation. Fruits such as plums and nectarines can easily replace cherries or peaches, and black currants or blackberries can replace our more common strawberries and raspberries.

Many exotic fruits, such as figs, kiwis, lichees and passion fruit are now much more readily available than they once were. Trying various combinations and proportions will turn creating your dessert into an adventure.

Vegetable Terminology

Like all great arts, cooking has developed its own vocabulary over its long history. As you will frequently find these terms, referring to both methods and dishes, in vegetables recipes, we thought it would be useful to offer descriptions of some of the most common ones.

Achar: A condiment composed of vegetables, fruit, and strong spices, marinated in vinegar.

Aillade: This term applies to preparations, usually vinaigrettes, made with a garlic base.

Bed: A layer of vegetables, noodles or rice covering the bottom of a platter, usually topped with meat and/or sauce.

Blanch: To plunge a vegetable briefly into boiling water and then cool it rapidly in cold water in order to peel it, to firm it up, to remove its acidity or to partially cook it before freezing.

Borsch: A thick creamy beet soup of Russian origin, frequently made with sour cream. Polish borsch has a cabbage base.

Braise: A method of slow cooking by simmering in a small quantity of liquid.

Brunoise: Vegetables cut into very small cubes.

Chiffonade: Leafy vegetables, such as lettuce, cut in very thin strips or ribbons.

Citronné: To rub the surface of certain fruits and vegetables with lemon juice to prevent discoloration from contact with air or with water during cooking.

Duxelles: A preparation of chopped mushrooms and either shallots or finely chopped onions, seasoned and moistened with white wine, and cooked over high heat. A demi-glace (brown sauce) is sometimes added to the reduced duxelles preparation. Frequently used as a filling for vegetables.

Eggplant Caviar: A purée of cooked eggplant, served with bread as an hors d'oeuvre.

Flute:	To cut small decorative grooves into vegetables or fruits.
Julienne:	Vegetables that have been cut into long thin strips.
Macédoine:	A combination of diced vegetables.
Minestrone:	An Italian soup made with rice (or pasta) and vegetables.
Mirepoix:	A preparation of carrots, celery and onions, cut into a large dice and added to various dishes to enhance their flavor.
Paysanne:	A mixture of finely chopped vegetables, used to prepare soups or to garnish meat, fish or omelettes.
Piperade:	A Basque dish consisting of beaten eggs combined with cooked tomatoes and peppers.
Pissaladière:	A savory tart made with tomatoes, anchovies, onions and black olives. It is similar to pizza.
Pistou:	A condiment characteristic of the cooking of Provence, made of fresh basil crushed with olive oil, garlic and grilled tomatoes and used in the preparation of certain vegetable dishes.
Primeurs:	Vegetables or fruit that can be obtained before their normal season of maturity.
Ratatouille:	A combination of zucchini, tomatoes, eggplant, onions, peppers and seasoning cooked in oil.
Scald:	The action of plunging fruit or vegetables into boiling water for a few seconds to facilitate removal of the skin. This method is very effective for peeling tomatoes.
Shell:	Extracting peas and beans from their shells.
Vert-pré:	A garnish of peas, asparagus tips and green beans that may be used with grilled meat or poultry dishes.

Culinary Terms

Have you ever been given a menu and found that you were unable to understand many of the words? In fact, many culinary terms tend to be rather obscure. Here is a short glossary of terms that may help you.

A la française: Vegetables, usually beans, which have been boiled, drained and coated in butter and lemon juice with chopped parsley.

Argenteuil: With asparagus tips as the main ingredient.

Basquaise: With ratatouille as the main ingredient.

Crécy: With carrots as the main ingredient.

Dubarry: With cauliflower as the main ingredient.

Duchesse: Potatoes that been peeled, boiled, drained, puréed and mixed with egg yolks and butter. They are formed into various shapes by hand or forced through a piping bag, brushed with butter and cooked in the oven.

Flamande: With Brussels sprouts as the main ingredient.

Florentine: With spinach as the main ingredient.

Parmentier: With potatoes as the main ingredient.

Provençale: With tomatoes, parsley and garlic as main ingredients.

Rachel: With artichokes as the main ingredient.

Saint-Germain: With peas as the main ingredient.

Soubise: With onions as the main ingredient.

Conversion Chart

Conversion Chart for the Main Measures Used in Cooking

Volume		Weight	
1 teaspoon	5 mL	2.2 lb	1 kg (1000 g)
1 tablespoon	15 mL	1.1 lb	500 g
		0.5 lb	225 g
1 quart (4 cups)	1 litre	0.25 lb	115 g
1 pint (2 cups)	500 mL		
1/2 cup	125 mL		
1/4 cup	50 mL	1 oz	30 g

Metric Equivalents for Cooking Temperatures

°C	°F	°C	°F
49°C	120°F	120°C	250°F
54°C	130°F	135°C	275°F
60°C	140°F	150°C	300°F
66°C	150°F	160°C	325°F
71°C	160°F	180°C	350°F
77°C	170°F	190°C	375°F
82°C	180°F	200°C	400°F
93°C	200°F	220°C	425°F
107°C	225°F	230°C	450°F

Readers will note that, in the recipes, we give 250 mL as the equivalent for 1 cup and 450 g as the equivalent for 1 lb and that fractions of these measurements are even less mathematically accurate. The reason for this is that mathematically accurate conversions are just not practical in cooking. Your kitchen scales are simply not accurate enough to weigh 454 g—the true equivalent of 1 lb—and it would be a waste of time to try. The conversions given in this series, therefore, necessarily represent approximate equivalents, but they will still give excellent results in the kitchen. No problems should be encountered if you adhere to either metric or imperial measurements throughout a recipe.

Index

A
Artichoke and Mushroom Salad. . 86
Asparagus with Almonds. 90

B
Baked Potatoes. 32
Beet Ketchup. 49
Beets with Vinegar. 48
Broccoli and Ham Casserole. 56
Broccoli with Almonds. 58
Brussels Sprouts with
   Mushrooms 59
Brussels Sprouts with
   Sour Cream. 60
Buying Vegetables. 10

C
Cabbage Quiche. 54
Carrots with Cream. 46
Casserole of Artichokes
   and Peas. 83
Cauliflower à la Polonaise. 60
Conversion Chart. 109
Cooking Fresh Vegetables. 17
Corn with Chili Sauce. 64
Culinary Terms. 108

D
Defrosting and Cooking
   Vegetables. 16

E
Entertaining 98
— Fruit and Pecan Tart. 105
— Green Salad. 104
— Lentil Soup. 100
— Tofu Quiche. 101

F
Freezing Vegetables. 14
Fried Vegetables Chinese Style. . . . 88
Fruit and Pecan Tart. 105

G
Garden Fresh Vegetables. 8
Glazed Carrots. 45
Green Beans with Tomato Sauce. . 62
Green Salad. 104

L
Leek Flan. 94
Lentil Soup. 100

M
Mixed Vegetables. 50

N
Note from the Editor. 6

O
Onion and Tomato Casserole. 78

P
Parsley Potatoes. 28
Potatoes with Onions. 40
Potatoes with Veal Stock. 34
Power Levels. 7

R
Ratatouille 66
Rutabaga and Green Pepper
   with Cheese. 53

S
Scalloped Potatoes. 36
Seasonal Vegetables. 12
Spinach Purée. 72
Stuffed Artichokes. 84
Stuffed Onions. 92
Stuffed Pepper Canapés. 80
Stuffed Potatoes. 30
Stuffed Zucchini. 68
Summer Vegetable Combination. . 96

T
Techniques for Preparing Fresh
   Vegetables. 20
Three-Vegetable Garnish. 42
Tofu Quiche. 101
Tomato Ketchup. 74
Tomato Mousse. 82
Tomatoes Provençale. 76
"Two-Step" Potatoes. 38

V
Vegetable Terminology. 106
Vegetables and the Microwave. . . . 26

Y
Yellow Beans Creole Style. 61

Z
Zucchini Italian Style. 70

MICROTIPS

For Perfectly Cooked
   Vegetables. 25
Determining Cooking Time
   or a Mixture of
   Vegetables. 29
For Best Results. 29
For Perfectly Cooked
   Potatoes 38
Making Smaller Quantities. . . 44
For a Quick Meal. 52
For Uniform Cooking. 57
About Salt. 63
Preparing Frozen Foods
   Quickly 65
To Defrost Small Servings of
   Vegetables. 79
To Clarify Butter. 89
To Keep Endive from
   Discoloring During
   Cooking 91
To Defrost Bread. 95
To Reheat Foods That
   Cannot Be Stirred. 97
Cutting Lettuce in
   Ribbons. 104